The Barefoot Way

DORI GRINENKO BAKER

The Barefoot Way

A Faith Guide for Youth, Young Adults, and the People Who Walk with Them

WESTMINSTER
JOHN KNOX PRESS
LOUISVILLE · KENTUCKY

First edition
Published by Westminster John Knox Press
Louisville, Kentucky

12 13 14 15 16 17 18 19 20 21—10 9 8 7 6 5 4 3 2 1

Book design by Drew Stevens
Cover design by designpointinc.com
Cover illustration: © Sureyya Akin/istockphoto.com

Library of Congress Cataloging-in-Publication Data
Baker, Dori Grinenko
    The barefoot way : a faith guide for youth, young adults, and the people who
walk with them / Dori Grinenko Baker.
        p. cm.
    ISBN 978-0-664-23802-5 (alk. paper)
    1. Christian youth—Religious life. I. Title.
    BV4850.B24 2012
    248.8'3—dc23

2011039950

Most Westminster John Knox Press books are available at special quantity
discounts when purchased in bulk by corporations, organizations, and special-
interest groups. For more information, please e-mail SpecialSales@wjkbooks.com.

CONTENTS

ACKNOWLEDGMENTS

I am deeply grateful to each of the storytellers who allowed a part of their lives to be present here. In the moments we gathered to be community with and for one another, we walked a barefoot path together, sensing God among us and growing finer for the experience. I will thank a few people by name here, but in truth the people who touched this book are too many to number. It wouldn't have emerged in this form, however, without the encouragement of Melissa Wiginton and Ulrike Guthrie. My collaborators at The Fund for Theological Education (FTE) — Stephen Lewis, James Goodman, Courtney Cowart, and Katie Oliff — all added their own insights as they read early drafts, particularly as we played with and settled on Stephen's acronym, L.I.V.E. Angie Seckler Williams and Jason C. Stanley, in addition to sharing their stories, were important collaborators. Others who made this work possible by sharing their stories, some of whom wish to remain anonymous, include Brenda T. Faison, Johnny Harkey, Mary Spencer, MK O'Haver, Kelly Wheeler, Aram Bae, Kathleen Lifsey, Debra McKune, Ellie Manspile, Melanie Sayre, Adrienne Better, and Adella Barrett.

I am grateful to numerous institutions that hosted me as an independent scholar over the past decade. They provided the most important ingredient: eager, engaged students of theology with a passion for youth and young adult ministry. The stories collected here emerged from the following sources: Project Burning Bush and master's degree courses at Union Presbyterian Seminary in Richmond, Virginia; the senior high youth of the Presbytery of the Peaks in Lynchburg, Virginia; the junior and senior high youth groups of Revielle United Methodist Church in Richmond, Virginia; and graduate courses at Methodist Theological School in Columbus, Ohio, and Wesley Theological Seminary in Washington DC. A special circle of teenage girls gave up their homecoming to create a retreat called Spa for the Girlfriend Soul at Smith Mountain Lake one fall weekend several years ago. That gathering was made possible through the gracious friendship of Minnie Bassett Lane and through a grant from the Valparaiso Institute, funded by the Lilly Endowment. The Lilly Endowment also makes possible the work of Calling Congregations and FTE as they support the next generation of leaders for the church.

I am also lucky to have a husband, Lincoln, who reminds me to pause, breathe, look up, and take in the joy of this moment. My daughters, Olivia and Erin, gift me daily with close-up glimpses of adolescent life, and they frequently remind me to kick off my flip-flops.

AN INVITATION

Remove the sandals from your feet,
for the place on which you are standing is holy ground.
— Exodus 3:5

My name is Dori Baker. I live in southern Virginia, where I am surrounded by trees and rivers. I like to coax spinach and arrugula out of the ground and will drop almost anything to go kayaking. I have two teen-aged daughters and am an ordained United Methodist minister. I also teach seminary courses and write about youth, young adults, and faith. This book grows out of a passion I've had for over a dozen years: looking for God in unexpected places, starting with a fresh, true story from someone's life.

When someone trusts a small group of people enough to share a personal story, we can almost feel the presence of God entering the room, sitting with us for a spell, and wandering with our imaginations into the story. Sometimes I wish I'd warned my companions with God's words to Moses: "Take off your shoes!" (Exod. 3:5, paraphr.) because time and again even the simplest of stories can lead us to an awed awareness that we're standing on holy ground. The stories in these pages come from people among whom I've stood on holy ground in retreats, seminary classrooms, churches, and interfaith workshops. Many of the writers have become my friends. The stories here are ones I hold close to my heart; I've kept in touch with the writers, and I've gotten their permission to share their stories with you. These stories reflect the places I've found myself over the past decade, which are mainline denominational churches and seminaries in which white people are still the majority. The stories here reflect that. I have included stories from African Americans and Asian Americans, but the careful reader will notice that a richer work would emerge from the inclusion of more nonwhite storytellers. For that reason, my story collecting goes on. As I continue to lead this process in places that are more reflective of the changing demographics of our nation and our religious worlds, I look forward to the emergence of a more intentionally inclusive collection.

If you discover a story of your own that you'd like to share, please do! You can send it to bakerdori@fteleaders .org, and we will consider using it for future volumes.

I hope that this book encourages you to take off your shoes, kick off your flip-flops, or step out of your stilettos. May it remind you to touch the holy ground on which you stand.

Is This Book for You?

This book is written for you if one of your primary memories of childhood is the collapse of the World Trade Towers. You may be in college. You may be working or looking for work. You may be taking a year off school to volunteer, to earn money, or to travel to Africa. You may be still in high school, thinking about what you'd like to do with the rest of your life. Or you may be simply living through this moment, not too concerned about the future. But wherever you are on your journey, this book comes with a simple invitation. Carry it with you for twenty-one days.

What this book is not:

— It's not packed with good advice.
— It does not promise to have all the answers.
— It's not edible.

What it is:

— It's as packable as an iPod, weighing only about seven ounces.
— It's a way to spend ten minutes a day tending your soul.
— It's a guide to listening for your inner voice.
— It's a reminder that your inner voice is often your best guide, connecting you to God's whispers and nudges, confirmed through quiet moments or in conversation with others.

This little book asks big questions about living a life that matters. It does that one little story at a time. The stories come from people like you—people who have glimpsed God (or whatever word you use to describe the Holy) in simple, everyday moments. When shared with a friend or circle of friends, these glimpses may point toward who you are and who you are becoming. Some of the stories will make you smile. Some will move you to text an old friend. Some will remind you of your own life—a loss of a loved one, a major disappointment, a heartbreaking end to a relationship, or a victory on the soccer field. Their purpose is to awaken in you the idea that your life is not as separate as it sometimes feels but that it is actually quite radically connected to the world and the people around you.

This book is also for you if one of your primary memories of childhood is Watergate or World War II. If you are an adult (of any age) who cares about teenagers and young adults, you may play a more important role than you know in the lives of young people, who face a lot of challenges in imagining a hope-filled future.

If you are a mentor, pastor, youth leader, parent or grandparent, this book can help you learn a simple, meditative practice for listening more intentionally to the young people in your midst. Young people need adults who don't have all the answers but are willing, like the poet Rainer Maria Rilke suggests, to "live the questions now" (*Letters to a Young Poet* [Novato, CA: New World Library, 2000]). Likewise, they need adults who are humble enough to remember, as theologian Howard Thurman suggests, that we all must take time to "listen for the sound of the genuine within us" (*The Spelman Messenger*, Summer 1980). Practicing the art of slowing down to listen to our lives is powerful at any stage of life. When we do so, we can begin to see the way our deeply felt values align with something new that wants to be born in the world. You may find your own passions reawakened as you explore this book alone or as you lead a group of young people. Ideas for ways of using this book with different ages and types of groups appear at the end of this section; tips for facilitating groups appear in an appendix at the end of the book.

Practicing the art of slowing down to listen to our lives is powerful at any stage of life. When we do so, we can begin to see the way our deeply felt values align with something new that wants to be born in the world.

What This Book Is About

Imagine yourself as part of God's ever-evolving world. "God's ecology" is a way of talking about the multiple, interconnected movements of God we can see working in and through the everyday realities of our life. Think of this book as a field guide to God's ecology. If you were walking a trail or kayaking a river near your home, you might carry with you a pocket-sized guide to help you identify the birds or plants you're likely to see. (If you're more of an urban hiker, think of the guide you would take through the streets of Barcelona or New Delhi, telling you where to direct your gaze to spot a Gaudí or where to find the best tandoori.) It helps you know what to look for and what to look at more closely once your attention's been grabbed.

In everyday life, each of us travels an inner landscape that intersects with our experiences in the world. Each inner landscape is unique, but when we share them, we discover common scenes. This field guide will help you track the landscape of your soul, pointing out scenes that might lead you to think, "Aha! I've been *there* before!" It will direct you toward places in the Bible and points of reference in Christian tradition as well as places where Christian beliefs find common ground with other faith traditions. It will point out places on the Web to learn more about ancient tools for faithful living that have been tested through the centuries and new ones emerging from creative souls traversing new territory. These will offer clues to help you reflect on the questions that matter about our place in God's world, such as

— What am I supposed to do with my life?
— What does God want of me?
— Which of my passions and gifts am I supposed to follow?
— What if what God seems to want of me is not what I want?
— Where do I look for signs that my life is on the right track?

— How do I find or create a community of others with whom to ask these questions?

— What do I do on the days when I can't remember what my passions and gifts are?

— Who is God? Who am I in God's eyes?

This field guide will help you track the landscape of your soul, pointing out scenes that might lead you to think, "Aha! I've been there before!"

Any of these questions might have been on the mind of young Moses that day when he was watching his father-in-law's sheep. He heard a voice telling him to take off *his* version of flip-flops, Nikes, Wallabees, Uggs, or Toms. Moses didn't ignore that voice. He looked up. He saw a burning bush. And the rest is history: Moses led a justice movement that reshaped God's story with humans and set the stage in so many ways for who Jesus Christ would reveal himself to be (Exod. 3:1–10).

How to Use This Book

Think about setting aside a certain time of the day to spend with this book. My sister keeps it in her bathroom and reads it while she's drying her hair. Maybe you will put it near your morning caffeine source or where you charge your phone: every time you drink or plug in can be a reminder to reconnect to your soul. It takes only a few minutes to step onto holy ground. When you come up from such a moment, you may find yourself more ready to respond to the ways God is bringing something new into the world through you.

In the following pages, you will find one person's real-life story for each day you use the book. The storytellers sometimes feel at home in their Christian tradition and sometimes at odds with it. They are sometimes trusting, sometimes doubtful. Some of the stories are funny. Some are tragic. Some of the stories are by people who are still in high school or middle school. Some are by adults, remembering back to their younger years. Many of these stories emerged from people who were on the path to becoming ministers—either ordained clergy, youth ministers, chaplains, or religious educators. But some of the storytellers are following different calls—to be involved in global peacemaking, for instance, or to dedicate their life to teaching, lab research, artistic expression, or social activism. Some of the storytellers are still in the middle of discerning their life's direction. The process of reflecting on these small stories is a way of tending to the larger story of their lives as they are unfolding. This larger story is sometimes called a vocation or calling: it usually becomes clear slowly over time, rather than in a sudden flash of lightning (or a burning bush).

It only takes a few minutes to step onto holy ground.

The L.I.V.E. Method

Each of the stories here has been told before—when the storyteller shared it with a group using a four-step process called L.I.V.E. The acronym L.I.V.E. spells out four steps to guide a short time of reflection (if you're alone) or conversation (if you're in a group). The steps are described in the next section. After you read each story, you will find a series of questions to walk you through the steps of L.I.V.E. Then you'll read what others gleaned from the same story.

Occasionally, there will be a day off. On these days, there is no story, because it is yours to write. Scan the inner landscape of your life experience. What is the story that pops into your mind? How would you tell it to a friend? Perhaps you'll use the space provided to write the story or draw a picture of it. Maybe you'll e-mail the story to a friend, tell it to a roommate, or share it with others who are reading this book with you. After recalling your story, you'll be guided through the steps of L.I.V.E. with it.

These four steps will help you remember a process of reflecting on the stories presented each day. Eventually, the steps can become second nature, and you may even come to think of them as ways of praying through life's everyday experiences. The L.I.V.E. process helps you seek direction from trusted others and to trust the inner voice of wisdom through which God speaks to you.

The L.I.V.E. Steps

The *L* reminds us to **LISTEN.** Breathe deeply, and allow yourself to be fully present to the story. Allow it to wash over you, as if you expect God to show up in it. Pay attention to the nuances, images, colors, smells, and sights in the

---

WHAT IS THEOLOGICAL REFLECTION?

Theological reflection describes the process of finding the overlap between our story and God's story. Through theological reflection, people discern the actions to which God may be calling them. Usually done in community, theological reflection is a hallmark of groups around the globe who have set out to change the world in order to make it a more faithful representation of God's *shalom* (the Hebrew word for God's vision of wholeness and peace).

story. Allow memories, feelings, and associations to come to mind as you enter the storyteller's world.

The *I* invites us to **IMMERSE** ourselves in the feelings the story evokes. As you identify feelings, name them. What emotions got stirred up in you? Talk about how the story made you feel: peaceful, afraid, excited, happy, nervous, anxious, joyful, blissful, frustrated, sad. A good way to uncover feelings is to pay attention to your body. Did your muscles tense? Did your eyes tear up? Did your breathing become shallow or speed up? These are signs that can lead to identifying your feelings, even if you can't quite put them into words. During this step, you may want to share a story from your own life that this story called to mind.

The *V* reminds us to **VIEW IT WIDER**: Take a step back from your feelings, and view the story wider, wondering about the images that grabbed you or the themes that seem central. What is this story about? How does this story remind you of God, either in your own faith tradition or from what you know about a different one? What story from the Bible, snippet of a sermon, or line from a song does it call to mind? Does it connect with a holy memory from your childhood, perhaps of a family gathering or another time when you felt completely and totally at home in the universe? Is there a Christian practice — such as welcoming the stranger, feeding the hungry, visiting those in prison, or offering praise — that it evokes? What does God look like to you as you ponder this story?

The *E* reminds us to **EXPLORE** actions and Aha! moments. Is there something about reflecting on this moment that you want to take forward with you into the day? Is there some action, small or large, you can imagine as a response to this story? Who does God want you to be in light of this story? The action might be as simple as naming an Aha! moment or declaring an intention, such as "I will look up to see the stars more often." Or it may be more costly, such as "I will commit to repairing a relationship that's broken," or "I will pay closer attention to the plight of illegal immigrants."

Now we're ready to proceed. The next time you pick up this book, there will be a story waiting for you.

A Note to Mentors, Youth Workers, Pastors, or Parents

This book comes to you from Calling Congregations, a movement to support the creative young people God is calling to lead the church and change the world. We believe that young people are hungry to create lives of meaning. We also believe that adults, when invited, make wonderful companions to youth who are searching. Such companionship requires creating space in which people can gather to share their lives and reflect together on God's often-mysterious presence. Out of such spaces might emerge

---

WHAT IS VOCATION?

Vocation is a word you'll see a lot in this book. For some it means what they do for a living; for others it means a divine call to professional Christian service. As I use it, *vocation* is not limited to either of those extremes. Instead, it points to the cluster of activities that give one's life purpose and meaning. I've written that "vocation is the practice through which people offer their lives in response to God's call, amid a world in need" (Dori Baker and Joyce Mercer, *Lives to Offer: Accompanying Youth on the Quest for Vocation* [Cleveland: Pilgrim Press, 2007], 8). I also like the way Walter Brueggemann says it: Vocation is "finding the purpose for your life that is part of the purposes of God" ("Covenanting as Human Vocation," *Interpretation* 33, no. 2 [April 1979]: 126).

wisdom and creativity needed for humans to flourish and to create a more sustainable world.

Congregations are ideal places for these kinds of conversations to happen, but we don't always know how to ask deep questions or to dive into more meaningful conversations, especially across generations. This book is part of a larger approach called VocationCARE that helps congregations, campus ministries, and other organizations nurture the inner lives of leaders (for more information, see www.fteleaders.org). The CARE in VocationCARE is an acronym that stands for

Creating hospitable spaces for conversation
Asking self-awakening questions
Reflecting theologically together
Enacting next faithful steps

This book can be a helpful tool to groups using the entire VocationCARE approach, but it can also stand alone. It's for individuals, face-to-face groups, and online networks who want to engage in the practice of reflecting theologically on their emerging vocation, call, and purpose. I hope it will guide people to reflect on how *their* dreams overlap

I hope it will guide people to reflect on how their dreams overlap with God's dream for the world.

with *God's* dream for the world. Out of such reflection will flow action—works of justice, care, and compassion that just might renew the church and change the world.

L.I.V.E. in Action

Over the past dozen years, I've shared this method with many different types of groups. Hearing specific ways others are using the practice might inspire you. Here are some of the ways L.I.V.E. is in action:

- A college campus minister created a L.I.V.E. group in which students meet weekly with older members of a local congregation. After a few weeks of learning the method through stories provided here, they began to take turns doing L.I.V.E. with a story from their own lives.
- A church youth group reads a story from the book during the first fifteen minutes of their Sunday night gatherings and then practices L.I.V.E. out loud together. Individuals in the group use the book as daily devotional reading during the week.
- An interfaith group of urban teens wanted a way to learn more about one another's different traditions. After learning the method, they adapted it to welcome explicitly the diverse images of the Holy that arise from various world religious, using stories from their own lives when they gather for monthly meetings.
- A group of young people preparing to enter seminary used L.I.V.E. to structure a series of online chats. It helped them prepare for the transition into seminary, surrounded by a community of supportive friends who had begun to know one another more deeply.
- A Sunday school teacher used the book to begin a season of learning for middle school students. He called students during the week, asking them to tell him a story that would be used the following Sunday. Each time a Bible story arose during the conversation, they would look it up using a concordance.
- Many groups (of young adults, youth, and mixed ages) involved in volunteer service have used L.I.V.E. to guide reflection on their own experiences

when they gather to support one another's activism with prayer and contemplation. Likewise, a group of young adults who have chosen to live in intentional community use it at the end of the day to reflect upon their work among their inner-city neighbors.

DAY ONE

The Hummingbird

By Jason, age twenty-six, remembering an event from his middle-school years

I had spent most of this warm summer day helping my mother clean, which is not something any middle-school, adolescent boy wants to do. I managed to escape with the phantom excuse of needing to take a walk. Once outside, I surprised myself by in fact setting off on a walk. Barefoot. Two paths led from our house to my grandparents' home across the creek. I chose the longer path that led through the woods behind my house, over the creek, and around the goat lot to the back field.

I took these walks often by myself during my adolescence. In high school, when faced with a difficult situation, I would take this same path to a large tree stump that became the place where I prayed. At another time in my life, I would walk this path for hours—worried, scared, and uncertain as to why my father had prostate cancer. But this day, I went for a walk just to get away from my mother for a few hours.

As I walked, I came upon the first creek to cross. I jumped over, being careful of the barbed wire attached to an oak tree to the left. I continued my walk. My right foot was in the air about to land securely on the ground when a noise caught my attention.

I looked down, uncertain why, to where my right foot was about to land. There on the ground was a small hummingbird. Awkwardly sidestepping the bird at the last moment, I knelt down to get a better look. How often does one get to see a hummingbird up close?

When I knelt down, I noticed that a piece of string was wrapped around the hummingbird. Unable to untangle itself, the bird was frightened and struggling. I tried to help, but the bird would not stay still.

I scooped it up with a piece of bark, and it slowly began to calm down. I hurried along the path. I came out at the back field and began to pick up speed, being careful not to drop the hummingbird.

I reached my grandparents' house just as they, keys in hand, were getting into the car to leave. I showed them the hummingbird. My grandfather went into his shop and came back with a pair of scissors. I thought for sure the hummingbird in its extreme excitement would prevent my grandfather from cutting the string.

To my surprise, the hummingbird remained calm. My grandfather snipped the string, untangling it from the hummingbird's wing. The hummingbird flew away.

Practice L.I.V.E.

Take a deep breath and close your eyes for a moment or two. **LISTEN** to the responses this story calls forth in you.

Now **IMMERSE** yourself in how this story made you feel. Did your body tense during part of the story and relax at another? Jot down the full range of feelings the story raised in you, from beginning to end. Of what stories from your own life did this story remind you? With whom or what in the story did you identify?

After you've sat for a few minutes with those feelings, begin to **VIEW IT WIDER**. Wonder where God is in the story. Is God at times like Jason, a youngster fleeing authority who is nonetheless attentive to a fellow creature in need? Is God the hummingbird, sometimes tangled up in discarded old meanings? What Bible stories or Christian practices does this story recall for you?

Finally, **EXPLORE** what there is about this story or the way it made you feel that you want to act on or continue pondering. What is there that helps you hear God speaking to your life today?

Take a moment to jot down answers to any of these questions and, especially, to remind yourself later of a story from your own life that this story called to mind.

What Others Experienced

When Jason shared this story with a group, childhood memories surfaced about special times spent with grandparents. A woman remembered the feeling of freedom she associates with being barefoot in the summertime. One man, who was feeling at odds with his faith tradition, identified with the trapped bird. He said he felt a small jolt of joy when the string was snipped.

As Jason and a few friends began to reflect about God in the story, Jesus' words "'He has sent me to proclaim release to the captives'" (Luke 4:18) came to mind. Jason got excited. He vividly retold his memory of the exact moment of release when the string was snipped and the hummingbird was freed. "It was so amazing," he said. "I thought for sure the bird would freak out, but he allowed us to get close."

WHAT IS A CHRISTIAN PRACTICE?

Christian practices are shared activities that, when woven together, form a faithful life. Christian practices have been embodied across the centuries and in different cultures, and many of them are now being reimagined for a new day. Prayer is a Christian practice, as is worshiping, feeding the hungry, caring for our bodies, caring for the earth, and providing hospitality. Christian practices "reflect and respond to God's grace to us and to the world in Christ," writes Dorothy C. Bass in *Practicing Our Faith: A Way of Life for a Seeking People* (San Francisco: Jossey-Bass, 1997). For more information, go to www.practicingourfaith.org, or check out the book *Way to Live: Christian Practices for Teens*, edited by Dorothy C. Bass and Don C. Richter (Nashville: Upper Room, 2002), 8.

As we came to the last step of L.I.V.E., Jason named a connection between this story, his desire to share it, and his call to be a part of God's "release of captives," which he imagines happening through his work as a youth minister. Another person in the group was struck by Jason's attentiveness to a small, defenseless creature and was drawn to remember the book of Genesis, God's creation of the world, and the Christian practice of caring for the earth and its creatures.

DAY TWO

Kick Off Your Flip-Flops

By Melissa, seventeen, recalling a recent event

Last Sunday I went to the labyrinth with Anne and Lisa. I kicked off my pink flip-flops. I felt the gravel pebbles under my feet. The sun was a hot presence above, making the humid air melt me. I stepped into the labyrinth and started running, sprinting, leaping along the paths, twisting, turning, doubling back, circling, centering. I stopped and lay down at the center of the labyrinth. The sky was a cloudy dream above me, with shapes and textures too intricate for words.

I stood and looked at the sky. Just then it started to rain. I looked at Anne, and she looked at me. We smiled. We twirled and skipped out of the labyrinth, delighting in living, ecstatic about simply being. I tumbled in the grass, and we cartwheeled. We spun in circles. The grass was slightly wet, but we didn't care. It was raining, and I was dancing.

Practice L.I.V.E.

Take a deep breath, and close your eyes for a moment or two. **LISTEN** to the responses the story calls forth in you.

Now **IMMERSE** yourself in the feelings evoked by the story. Can you remember a time like this in your life—a day or a moment when you felt connected to the creator of the universe or to someone or something else? Did an image stand out for you? Of what stories from your own life did this story remind you? With whom or what in the story did you identify?

After you've sat for a few minutes with those feelings, begin to **VIEW IT WIDER.** Open to God, wondering where you might name God's presence in the story. Of which psalm or other Scripture does it remind you? How do you sense God here . . . as the creator of the spinning planet or as the giver of raindrops, cartwheels, and friendships? Do you have a sense of the ways God awakens you through experiences of awe, wonder, and ecstasy?

Now **EXPLORE** if there is an action or an Aha! moment for you here. What is there about this story or the way it made you feel about yourself or God that you want to act on or continue pondering?

What is there about this story and your reflection on it that helps you hear God speaking to your life today? Take a moment to jot down answers to any of these questions and, especially, to remind yourself of a story from your own life that this story called to mind.

What Others Experienced

After listening to Melissa's story, a circle of her friends shared their memories of other times when a crystal clear, sparkling moment occurred, smack in the middle of everyday life. We talked about the Gospel story of the transfiguration, when Jesus was walking up a mountain with his friends, and all of a sudden there was something older people would describe as "an inbreaking of glory." In this moment, they saw Jesus not just as a wandering teacher

WHAT IS A LABYRINTH?

Many people think of a labyrinth as a convoluted maze, but it is actually a physical form of prayer dating back to medieval times when it was dangerous for people to make pilgrimages to the Holy Land. In walking a labyrinth, you can't get lost: it's *not* a maze. Your path on a labyrinth is a lot like life: it takes many twists and turns, often bringing you back close to the beginning just when you seem to be getting to the end. Ultimately, the labyrinth leads you safely to the center, then back out into the world. Walking a labyrinth is a way of praying with your body, mind, and spirit. It is a way of centering or symbolically making a pilgrimage while staying close to home. Labyrinths can be found in many communities—at churches, hospitals, universities, and parks. You can find one in your part of the world through www.labyrinthlocator.com. Portable labyrinths are sometimes set up in churches or at large gatherings. View some at www.fhlglobalministries.org. Learn to make your own at www.lessons4living.com/drawing. Find out more by reading *Walking a Sacred Path* by Lauren Artriss (New York: Riverhead Books, 1995).

or a carpenter's son but as God's son, his face shining like the sun and his clothes a dazzling white (Matt. 7:1–9). Peter wanted to freeze the moment, to make it permanent by constructing a dwelling in which to house it. We talked about how moments of feeling so radically connected to God and one another are usually fleeting. Telling someone about them is a way of making them more permanent. By revisiting them we name them as sacred and are reminded of God's abiding presence even long after the experience of God is gone.

We talked about the temptation to be busy, to be so wrapped up in thinking about what's going to happen next that we miss the moment in which we're living now. It's so easy to miss the present moment, especially when one feels

WHAT IS A MANTRA?

A mantra is a simple phrase, sometimes uttered as a prayer, that can keep our hearts and minds centered. Although the term is commonly associated with Eastern religions, Christians have also been using mantras since ancient times. Perhaps you can create a mantra from your life experience that helps you remember to be open to God's presence in the ups and downs of your daily life and in the larger arcs of your personal history. Some people use a few lines of a psalm as a mantra, such as "Be still and know that I am God" (Ps. 46:10).

burdened by questions or concerns about the future. One woman said our reflection on the story would change her behavior: "I will *always* kick off my flip-flops and enjoy the raindrops with a friend," she said. "This story reminds me to live the moment I am given."

It wasn't until much later, while reflecting on this conversation, that I heard in it an echo of God telling Moses to take off his sandals at the burning bush. "Kick off your flip-flops" became a daily mantra, reminding me to be on the lookout for moments when God might be wanting my attention.

DAY THREE

Dancing with Thelma

By Johnny, age sixteen, recalling a recent event

On our first weekend together, we went to a bluegrass concert at a local retirement center. Up until that point we had all just been hanging out, getting to know one another, and I was wondering how I would carry over the energy from being with people my own age to being with older folks. When we all got to the retirement center, I decided that I would goof around and dance my way to the refreshment table. While I was doing that, a woman, who looked to be about eighty years old, jumped up and started to dance with me. She was really cuttin' a rug for her age. She was so full of life!

Here's the kicker: I learned later that she had just been cleared to be active after having hip-replacement surgery. It was absolutely amazing! Dancing with Thelma gave me so much joy. I saw God radiating through her.

Practice L.I.V.E.

After you've read Johnny's story, take a deep breath, and close your eyes for a moment or two. **LISTEN** to the responses it calls forth in you.

Now **IMMERSE.** Recall your feelings. What did this story bring to mind for you? Think of a time when you connected with someone who was not your age. Perhaps it was with an older person like Thelma. Perhaps it was with someone much younger than you. What did it feel like? Does it happen to you often?

After you've sat for a few minutes with those feelings, **VIEW IT WIDER** by beginning to wonder where God is in the story. Does it remind you of a passage of Scripture? Or perhaps a hymn, camp song, or a praise song?

Now **EXPLORE** actions it might call forth. Ask yourself if there is an Aha! moment for you here? Is there something about this story or the way it made you feel about yourself or God that you want to act on or to continue pondering?

What is there about this story and your reflection on it that helps you hear God speaking to your life today? Take a moment to jot down answers to any of these questions and, especially, to recall a story from your own life that this story called to mind.

What Others Experienced

When Johnny finished reading this story to a group of friends, smiles broke out everywhere. As we began naming our feelings, Mike talked about how happy he was that Johnny had made eye contact: he noticed Thelma, and they danced. He could have ignored her or just nodded politely, and if he had, the moment never would have happened.

When talk turned to God, someone mentioned King David, dancing his undignified dance in front of the Ark of the Covenant, a vessel considered holy by the ancient Israelites (Ps. 30:11–12). We talked about Thelma's little moment of celebration being like the words in that psalm: "You have taken off my sackcloth and clothed me with joy." There are times to be undignified, we laughingly acknowledged. We also talked about Miriam's song—that moment of celebration that erupted after the exodus people had crossed safely to the other side of the Red Sea (Exod. 15:20–21). Thelma, too, had just crossed over a dangerous terrain. There are times to celebrate boldly, we agreed, without stopping to worry too much about the ongoing risk.

When I asked if there was an "Aha! moment"—one way in which this snapshot of Johnny and Thelma dancing would stick with anyone—Mike jumped in. "I'll forever think of *this*—this joy, this connection, this gift—when I hear the words 'intergenerational fellowship,'" he said. Mike went on to name an action he would incorporate into his life because of Johnny's story and our reflection on it. "I'll try to stay open to moments like these," he said. "It would have been a shame if Johnny had politely nodded at Thelma, been embarrassed by the encounter, and walked away."

MORE ABOUT THEOLOGICAL REFLECTION

Theological reflection happens when we look for the place where our stories meet up with God's story. It's central to the movement of L.I.V.E. we're experiencing in this book, and it happens all the time: in church when a preacher ties a personal experience to a passage from Scripture; at a funeral, when the Twenty-third Psalm is read and imagined through the particulars of the life of the one who has died; on Easter morning, when we go to a sunrise service, hear the story we know by heart, and feel our own brokenheartedness over life's Good Fridays mended in a glimpse of resurrection. It can also happen in the car on the way home from a track meet or around the family dinner table: seeing where God is in our day is a practice that we get better at the more we do it.

DAY FOUR

Your Story

Write your name and a brief description of yourself in the space provided below.

Next is a space for an image of you. Paste a photo, if you want. But if you feel otherwise inspired, doodle a depiction of who you are today. Maybe it's a minicollage of symbols representing what you care about. Maybe it's an abstract set of lines or squiggles into which you can gaze for a few minutes and find yourself reflected.

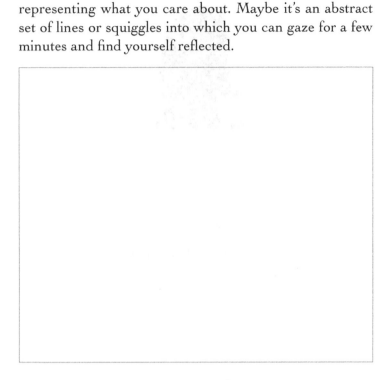

Now Try This

Look lovingly at the image of yourself. Imagine seeing yourself through the eyes of God. Breathe deeply, and really settle into this moment.

Immerse yourself in the emotions that emerge when you think of yourself in relationship to God. Do you feel comforted, doubtful, connected, peaceful, afraid, lonely?

View yourself wider, imagining a story from Scripture that comes to mind when you gaze at your image in relation with God. Do you remember the moment in Scripture when God said of Jesus, "You are my beloved child, in whom I am well pleased" (Mark 1:11)? Imagine God seeing you, just as you are right now, whispering those words to you. (You may not feel that way *at all*. That's absolutely fine. See if you can come up with an image from Scripture that *does* connect with how you feel right now, in this moment.)

Explore actions that might arise from your feelings. Is there some small action you'd like to make today in response to God's call in your life? Attend to any Aha! moments that arise for you.

What story from your life comes to mind after imagining yourself through God's eyes? We've done theological reflection about Jason and the hummingbird, Melissa and her pink flip-flops, and Johnny dancing with Thelma. Is there a glimpse from your own life that one of these stories brought to mind? If so, write it here:

_____

_____

_____

_____

_____

Find a friend, mentor, or family member. Ask that person to listen to your story. Then together consider the L.I.V.E. questions that have followed each story:

_____

_____

_____

_____

_____

Practice L.I.V.E.

LISTEN to the details of your own story. Pretend you're listening with God's ears.

IMMERSE yourself in how the story makes you feel. Then **VIEW IT WIDER** to wonder where God is in the story and to see your feelings or associations around it.

EXPLORE any Aha! moments in the story, and consider how you might act as a result of hearing and reflecting on this story.

UNTOLD STORIES

"What if I don't have a story?" "What if my story is too painful?" These are both responses I sometimes hear when I ask people to share a story. A few years ago, my youngest daughter couldn't imagine what story she would tell. We talked about an incident that happened during recess the year before, when someone excluded one of her friends from a game on the basis of skin color. We talked about another time when she looked out the window and saw an albino deer, thought by some native tribes to be a sign of God's favor. We all have stories that are ripe for theological reflection. But some of our stories are very sad. Once a woman told me that her story was too painful for her church friends to hear. I reminded her that our Christian story is centered in the pain of an unjust execution. If, as Christians, we cannot sit with one another through the most painful stories our lives hold, who can? Even though your story might be painful, I urge you to keep trying until you find a listening ear. For, as Zora Neal Hurston, a novelist of the Harlem Renaissance, writes in *Dust Tracks on the Road*: "There is no agony like bearing an untold story within you" (New York: HarperCollins, 1942).

DAY FIVE

The Bus

By MK, age twenty-four, recalling high school

I can remember the feeling of dread every weekday morning my freshman year of high school. The anxiety every Sunday night was overwhelming, as I worried over the inevitable morning. I felt joy and relief flood through me every Friday when I knew I had two whole days when I wouldn't have to ride the bus.

The bus. The bane of my freshman existence. Until one day.

I stood by the curb in front of my house, tired from a night of worry and hungry because I hadn't been able to eat breakfast, shivering as much from the fear as from the cold. I could always hear the bus as it rumbled around the corner and onto my street. It loomed in my vision like a train bound for hell. The brakes screeched as it stopped in front of me. The doors belched as they opened. The three steps led me up into the cavernous tube of torture filled with a sea of unfriendly faces. With a slam and a lurch, the big yellow bus pitched me into the gauntlet.

Every seat was full. Several had a third student perched on the edge. I searched each row for a friendly face. Heck, an apathetic face would have worked, too! I lumbered down the aisle wanting nothing more than some place to sit for the ten-minute ride. Eyes would dart to the windows. Heads would drop. The few eyes that would meet mine were threatening. Words would fly: "No way." "Forget it." "Move on, fatty."

I stopped three-quarters of the way back. There were no seats in front of me: that was where the seniors sat. No underclassmen sat back there without invitation. I slowly turned, hoping I had missed some edge of a seat. Again, words flew: "You can't sit here." "You'll squash us." "Freshman."

As if my daily humiliation wasn't enough, this day the seniors were going to get in on it, too. My cheeks reddened. Tears glistened in my eyes. The bus rumbled on. I turned, not sure what to do, when I heard a voice say, "Come sit with us! Ignore those pieces of sh-t. We know you're all right. Sit here!" And I did, that day and every day.

Practice L.I.V.E.

After you've read MK's story, take a deep breath, and close your eyes for a moment or two. **LISTEN** to the responses it calls forth in you. What clues might your body be giving you to help you identify your feelings about this story? Goose bumps, tightened muscles, increased heart rate, and faster breathing can all be signs that the story affected you at a level of which you might not be immediately aware.

Now **IMMERSE** yourself in your feelings, and share them. Did you climb inside MK's fear and apprehension as it builds in anticipation of Monday? Did you empathize with her long walk filled with unfriendly faces? Did you hope for an ending like this, or did it take you by surprise?

Jot down the full range of feelings the story raised in you, from beginning to end. Of what stories from your own life did this story remind you? With whom or what in the story did you identify?

After you've sat for a few minutes with those feelings, begin to **VIEW IT WIDER**. Wonder where God is in the story. Where do you think God is when people are suffering? In what ways are you aware of human suffering, close to home or across the globe? How do you think God hears our prayers in the midst of suffering? What Bible stories or Christian practices does this story recall for you?

After sitting for a while with the **LISTEN, IMMERSE,** and **VIEW IT WIDER** steps, ask yourself if there is an Aha! moment or action for you here. What is there about this story or the way it made you feel about yourself or God that you want to continue pondering? What is there about this story and your reflection on it that helps you hear God speaking to your life today? To what action does it point? Take a moment to jot down answers to any of these questions and, especially, to remind yourself later of a story from your own life that this story called to mind.

What Others Experienced

Listeners immediately empathized with MK's position of being the outsider. Almost everyone recalled a memory from adolescence of fearing or feeling hurtful exclusion. Tammy expressed her frustrations—begun in childhood but continuing far her into adulthood—about times when she felt she was judged by outward appearances rather than being honored and known for who she really is.

We made connections between the oppression MK felt from others' responses to her being overweight and the exclusion often experienced by people because of their skin color, immigrant status, sexual orientation, or even something as seemingly trivial as a bad case of acne. Then talk turned to the person who has the courage to speak up on behalf of one who is suffering.

Who was that compassionate senior? What called her to notice MK's distress and speak up? Where did the words come from? From whom or what had she learned this compassion and this ability to dare to counter the group's thinking? In this instance, that welcome had huge repercussions — memories that lasted for decades and continue to inspire MK toward acts of hospitality and inclusion.

When we turned to wondering what Scripture this story called to mind, someone vaguely remembered a passage about treating strangers with hospitality, because we were once strangers ourselves. This seemed to connect with the almost universal experience of being the outsider or the excluded one. We couldn't remember the passage exactly, so we used a concordance to look it up. We found Exodus 23:9, which says, "You must not oppress the strangers; you know how a stranger feels, for you lived as strangers in the land of Egypt."

From here, we noted the consistent strain through both the Hebrew Bible (sometimes called the Old Testament) and the New Testament that shows God's compassion for those who are suffering and oppressed. This led us to a discussion of the story of the Good Samaritan (Luke 10: 25–37) and then to the story Jesus tells about judging people based on

---

WHAT IS A CONCORDANCE?

A concordance is a book that helps you look up Scripture passages based on key words. In this case we looked up the words "alien" and "stranger" to find the passage we were thinking about. An online concordance can be found at www.eliyah.com/lexicon.html. Many study Bibles have concordances in the back.

their compassion (Matt. 25:35–46). While MK wasn't literally in prison, it was easy to see how she was imprisoned by her dread and the coldness of her classmates. Pondering this story made several people claim an Aha! moment that went like this: "It's not so important to figure out whose side God is on. The important question is 'How do I stand on God's side?'" We saw in this moment that life gives many opportunities to stand, as Jesus often did, on the side of the downtrodden, be that on a school bus, in a lunchroom, or on behalf of a child soldier in Darfur.

DAY SIX

Flying

By Mary, age twenty-four, recalling a memory from high school

I am flying. The warm breeze hits my face as I circle the crowds and the noise below. My arms at my sides, I don't have to worry about falling, or what I look like, or what I'm doing with my life. When I'm flying, I don't have to worry about anything at all.

Minutes before, I was a part of the sea of faces below. I am with two friends at the local fair, where we're spending too much money and riding the not-so-safe rides. We carpool to Salem, singing along to Broadway musicals in my friend's cool, purple car, stopping for fast food on the way. When we arrive, it looks like rain, but that doesn't bother us at all. We're running from the Ferris wheel to the haunted house to the roller coaster in our ponchos, laughing and giggling like we are eight years old again. With cotton candy sticking to my mouth and a smudge of ketchup on my friend's lip, we try our luck at the ring toss and the squirt guns. I get mildly insulted at what the guy thinks that I weigh, but I am now the proud owner of an orange stuffed frog for my brief embarrassment. We ridicule the lameness of the haunted house, but all three of us jump when the ride operator lunges toward us at the end. We ooh and aah over the acrobats dressed as pirates, briefly wondering what exactly it would be like to be a Columbian pirate performing at the Salem fair. We taste samples of food the local grocery store is giving away and declare all of the art projects we are going to accomplish as we peruse the craft exhibit. We attempt the large slide with potato sacks and decide it's not meant for people with hips. We watch the dancing elephants, and then pay for a ride. We are just as excited, if not more so, than the small children riding with us, and we proudly sport our "I rode an elephant!" stickers. We *must* buy a funnel cake, because that's just what you eat at the fair. We swear that we won't ride the whirling rockets right after we polish off said funnel cake, and then we do it anyway. We walk around holding our stomachs for the next half hour.

We are such good friends that not much needs to be said as we enjoy the improving weather, the rides, the food, and hanging out without a care in the world. We joke that we are already planning our scrapbook pages as we take random pictures throughout the day. Before we leave, my friends indulge my deep need to ride the swings, so we clip in, and the ride begins.

And then, I am flying. The sounds, colors, and people below blend together as I lift my feet in front of me, gently moving up and down as we spin high above the county fair. Life isn't complicated up here. I am just flying. The fun and friendship that have filled my day surround me as I glide above the tents and the people below. I can see the mountains in the distance as the sun disappears, leaving me zooming in the dusk above the crazy light and colors below. I can hear snippets of different songs blasting from the booths below; each would take me to a different place if I listened carefully and sang along. But no soundtrack is needed up here. Just the wind in my ears as I stare into the dark.

I know that soon the ride will end. I will have to return to earth, leave the fair, and go home. But for now, I am flying.

Practice L.I.V.E.

After you've read Mary's story, breathe. Close your eyes. Stretch. **LISTEN** to your body as you call forth the images from the story that remain with you.

Now **IMMERSE** yourself in the story. Could you smell the funnel cakes? Hear the music? Feel the wind in your face? Did your body tense during one part of the story and relax at another? Jot down the full range of feelings the story raised in you, from beginning to end. Then think about stories from your own life that this story calls to mind. Remember a time when you floated past adult burdens and could actually feel childlike abandon. Recall the feeling, if only for a moment, of not having a care in the world. Can you revisit a memory of a time of easeful flow with a friend?

After you've sat for a few minutes with those feelings, begin to **VIEW IT WIDER** as you wonder where God is in the story. How is God like a pair of good friends who sometimes take us to a place of letting go, a place of relaxed, carefree being? How does God entice us back to childlike awe? Where is God in the tension between everyday responsibilities and occasional moments of pure bliss? What story from the Bible comes to mind?

After sitting for a while with the **LISTEN, IMMERSE,** and **VIEW IT WIDER** steps, ask yourself what you can **EXPLORE** here. What is there about this story or the way it made you feel about yourself or God that you want to continue pondering? What is there about this story and your reflection on it that helps you hear God speaking to your life today? Is there an action it is calling forth? Take a moment to jot down answers to any of these questions and, especially, to remind yourself later of a story from your own life that this story called to mind.

What Others Experienced

When Mary told her story, there were smiles on all the faces of the other young-adult volunteers who listened. They shared memories of similar unexpectedly fun and carefree days. One person mentioned how relaxed she became as she allowed herself to sit, breathe, and listen to Mary's story, reliving the memories it called forth. Mia shared a deep ache of longing for good friends that came to mind during Mary's story.

As we played with the image of flying high above the carnival, two stories from Scripture arose. The first was of Jesus welcoming the children. In her story, Mary says she feels like she is eight again. Jesus tells the crowd, through his words and actions, that children belong in the world he is bringing to birth. Being childlike for a day seems to be connected to the simplicity of faith Jesus asks for in Mark 10:14–16.

Someone pointed to the story of the transfiguration told in Mark 9:2–9. In a flash, Jesus and his disciples were lifted out of the ordinary world and put in a place where they could see everything clearly, if only for a moment.

There is a sense in both of these stories of gaining a new perspective, a new way of seeing the world. Most often, we see it "from below," as does a small child looking up at the adult world. But occasionally, we seem to get glimpses "from above" as did these adults who relived with childlike excitement the experience of flying.

In the story of the transfiguration, the disciples want to erect a memorial to the moment, but our storyteller Mary knows, as Jesus knew, that she must "go back down the mountain." She must return to the responsibilities of the world below. Yet when she does, she returns with a different perspective. "I could see everything clearly from above, what's important and what's not," she said, which reminded her of the story of God's call of Moses. In it, God says, "'Remove the sandals from your feet, for the place on which you are standing is holy ground'" (Exod. 3:5). A moment later, God directs Moses' gaze away from this mountaintop experience back down to the earth below, saying, "'I have observed the misery of my people who are in Egypt; I have heard their cry on account of their taskmasters. Indeed, I know their sufferings, and I have come

CLEARNESS COMMITTEES

There's a little book called *Let Your Life Speak: Listening for the Voice of Vocation* written by a Quaker writer and teacher named Parker J. Palmer (San Francisco: Jossey Bass, 2000). Palmer reflects on some issues raised by Mary's story. Particularly, he tells about how his own vocation emerged in fits and starts through college and beyond. He beautifully describes a Quaker practice called a clearness committee, in which a circle of trusted friends helps a person discern the next steps in his life's journey.

Although Mary's friends in this story don't look anything like a Quaker clearness committee, they do symbolize the kind of trusting friendships that can allow God's in-breaking Spirit to appear as the most natural thing in the world, smack in the middle of everyday life. For more information about clearness committees and Palmer's work go to www.couragerenewal .org/parker/writings/clearness-committee.

down to deliver them'" (Exod. 3:7–8). We pondered this movement. We wondered about God's giving us moments of clarity, moments in which we can almost taste, touch, and smell the reign of God. These moments are often followed by ones that demand we hit the ground running, times when we are once again immersed in the day-to-day struggles, worries, and concerns of ourselves and the people we love and serve. When this event occurred in Mary's life, she was in the midst of decisions about how she would use her life for God's purposes. This "day apart" filled with friendship, childlike joy, and connection to the world below refreshed and refueled Mary for the work of figuring out her next steps in life.

DAY SEVEN

My First Dirty Word

By Aram, age twenty-seven, thinking back to her elementary school years

Michael was my friend only because we lived in the same apartment building. He wasn't the kind of person a third-grader wants as a friend. He was chubby and awkward. I'm pretty sure I talked to him only when we walked to school in the mornings or back home in the afternoons. I wanted to be friends with the popular kids. That meant the pretty kids, the slender kids, and the kids with new sneakers. Because I was the only Asian kid at my school, I was always trying to fit in. Today was my chance.

It was recess time. For once, we weren't playing with our jump ropes. Today the boys and girls played together. We played tag, except the boys were the only ones catching and grabbing the girls. I don't remember how I was invited to play, but I remember playing with the popular kids—even the fourth graders! I was screaming, smiling, and happily running around when a fourth-grade boy grabbed me. He locked his arms around me. I was still screaming and smiling with joy. A fourth-grade boy had

29

his arms around me! Then, he told me to say the "s" word. His voice was quiet enough so that the teachers couldn't hear us but loud enough that Michael heard.

The older boy kept saying, "Say it, and I'll let you go! Say it!" I don't know what Michael was thinking, but he ran over and yelled back, "Don't say it! Don't say it!" Literally, in one ear I heard the older boy coaxing me to say the "s" word, and in the other ear I heard Michael yelling loudly, "Don't say it!" Michael's voice was loud, but the boy's grip was firmer, and I was still smiling. So I said it. I said the "s" word. The boy let me go. I was free to run around and eagerly wait for the next boy to grab me.

I looked up, ready to start screaming so that the other boys knew I was free to tag. I saw Michael just staring at me. He said, "I'm going to tell our teacher on you!" I was scared. I begged him not to say anything, but I was sure he would.

Recess was over, and we went back to our classroom. I was waiting for the teacher to call on me, to send me to the principal's office, but it never happened. On our way home from school, I promised Michael I would never say the "s" word again.

Practice L.I.V.E.

After you've read Aram's story, take a deep breath, and close your eyes for a moment or two. **LISTEN** to the responses it calls forth in you.

Now **IMMERSE** yourself in your feelings. Share the embodied memories this story brings to mind. Can you smell the sweaty bodies on the playground? Do you remember the excitement of playing tag? Does the story bring back pleasant or unpleasant memories? With whom or what in the story did you identify? Note the full range of emotions you feel when you listen to this story or remember your elementary school self.

After you've sat for a few minutes with those feelings, begin to **VIEW IT WIDER.** Wonder where God is in the story. Is there a story from Scripture that seems to speak to you? Where is God when we are trying to fit in? Or when we struggle with competing desires? Is God in the loyalty Michael showed or in the moment of grateful surprise when Aram learned Michael had kept her secret?

EXPLORE any Aha! moments. What is there about this story or the way it made you feel about yourself or God that you want to act on or to continue pondering?

What is there about this story and your reflection on it that helps you hear God speaking to your life today? Take a moment to jot down answers to any of these questions and, especially, to remind yourself later of a story from your own life that this story called to mind.

What Others Experienced

After listening to Aram's story, the group launched into flashbacks associated with the sights, smells, and sounds of their elementary school playgrounds. Who would have guessed playgrounds carry so many emotionally laden memories? Some people laughed at the seriousness associated with first saying a "bad" word. Others identified with the rush of adrenalin and the sense of aliveness out on the playground in contrast to school-aged memories of the cooped-up feeling of young bodies in classrooms. For others, the playground recalled feelings of exclusion and shame, especially for those who could connect with Aram's position as an ethnic minority. In response, Aram shared that on the weekends at church she knew who she was and that she belonged. School was a very different world, a world in which she felt excluded but to which she badly wished to belong. "I remember an overwhelming feeling of wanting to blend in," she said.

This feeling of living in two different worlds was often accompanied by an inexplicable sense of shame for Aram. This caused a member of the group to wonder if there was a connection between Aram's story and Peter's denial of Jesus in the hours after his crucifixion (Mark 14:66–72). Like Aram, Peter wanted to blend in to the crowd. He didn't want to stand out; he was like a person living in two different worlds. Perhaps he felt shame after the denial. Jesus, the friend who visited and comforted Peter after the resurrection, points to a God who hangs around with us, even in the midst of our shame over real or perceived failures.

When we talked about Michael's choice *not* to tell the teacher and to walk home with Aram at the end of the day, an Aha! moment emerged. "If I am feeling ashamed, it doesn't mean I'm not in the presence of God. I can be in the presence of God and still feel shame," Aram said. Michael's abiding presence was reminiscent of the kind of God who hangs around, even when we don't feel we are worth hanging around with.

When in your life did someone "walk you home," even though you didn't feel like you deserved it? How might

COMING-OF-AGE MOMENTS

Aram's story illustrates a particular coming-of-age moment in the life of a person who had to learn at an early age to navigate borders of race and ethnicity. This shaped her in ways she now sees as important in her vocation as a religious educator. If these themes are interesting to you, you might want to check out one of Aram's favorite young-adult novels about the Asian/American experience, *A Step from Heaven* by An Na (New York: Penguin, 2001). You can learn more about the author, who was born in Korea and grew up in San Diego, at www.anwriting.com/author.html.

God love the parts of us that hold shame, even as God urges us to move beyond shame? Is there a way in which God calls you to be a Michael, standing alongside someone who's having difficulty knowing who they are and what their purpose is?

DAY EIGHT

Stars

*By Kathleen, age nineteen, recalling a memory from late
high school*

So you know when you just have one of those crappy
weeks? Nothing is going your way. You're getting bom-
barded with homework that can't possibly all get done.
Your friends are angry with you. You can't sleep at night
because you're worrying about everything. You know, one
of those kinds of weeks? Yeah, I was having one of those
weeks last winter.

I could not wait for the weekend to come so that I could
catch up on sleep, homework, and hang-time with my
friends. My parents were going out of town for a night, so
my best friend, Yasmine, was spending the night with me.
A mutual friend of ours, Joseph, convinced the two of us
to come hang out with him. We decided to be spontaneous
and adventurous, not even knowing where or what we were
going to do. We bundled up and went to pick up Joseph.

He was hungry, so we stopped for fast food. Then we
were just driving around town, talking and having a good
time. All of a sudden, Joseph announced that he had a

"brilliant" idea. Typically, whenever Joseph says that, we prepare for something extravagant, overcomplicated, far too risky, or just plain dumb. He asked me if I trusted him—a bad sign—and I said yes, even as I thought to myself, "Oh boy, here we go." He told me just to drive where he directed, and I complied.

Off we went, onto the highway, off an exit, and finally winding along an old country road. We arrived at a gravel lane that curved up a steep mountain.

"Are we seriously going to drive up this?" I asked.

"Yes, we are, indeed!" replied Joseph enthusiastically.

"Yasmine, are you going to be okay with this?" I asked, concerned about her tendency to get carsick.

"I suppose. It just better be worth it when we get to the top," she said.

"Oh, it most certainly will!" exclaimed Joseph.

So on I drove in my little 1994 silver Volvo sedan, slowly winding up the mountain. We got to a field. Joseph told me to pull off the road into a small driveway. He got out, and we followed.

There was nothing. We were standing in a hilly field with weeds growing everywhere, trees outlining the field, a couple of dilapidated barns, and the freezing air nipping at our faces. I was unimpressed.

"Now look up," Joseph instructed us. We did.

The sky was filled end to end with twinkling stars. There was not a cloud in the sky. It was amazing. All was silent except for us breathing into our cupped hands to warm them.

"Do you want a better view?" he asked.

We both nodded silently, still gazing at the sky.

"Get back in the car, and let's go."

We followed the small driveway higher up the mountain. We pulled up in front of a quaint little wooden frame house. Joseph told us that this was where his older sister lived with her husband. He had called ahead to tell her that we were coming. She was already waiting on the porch for us, blankets in hand. We climbed out of the car and ran to bundle ourselves up even more. I stood on the porch and looked to my left.

There was a break in the surrounding forest that was lining their yard. There lay the city of Lynchburg. It was glowing. The lights of downtown illuminated the taller buildings. There were smaller, dimmer streetlights scattered about the outskirts. Blanketing this astounding sight was the sky. It was the same cloudless sky we had seen ten minutes ago, but with *more* stars. All was silent. I sank into the porch swing, admiring the sight before me, allowing my body and mind to feel the peace. My friends sat down beside me. All the worry, all the pain, all the stress, all the anxiety . . . everything just melted away.

It was just me, the stars, my friends, the cold air, and the city lights. It was breathtaking.

Practice L.I.V.E.

After you've read Kathleen's story, take a deep breath and close your eyes for a moment or two. **LISTEN** to the responses it calls forth in you, and **IMMERSE** yourself in the feelings.

Now try to name your feelings. Did you worry, as Kathleen did, about what tragic end the mysterious journey might lead to? Did you feel excitement or apprehension as the car wound up the curvy mountain road? Jot down the full range of feelings the story raised in you, from beginning to end. Of what stories from your own life did this story remind you? With whom or what in the story did you identify?

After you've sat for a few minutes with those feelings, begin to **VIEW IT WIDER**. Wonder where God is in the story. How is God at times like Kathleen's friend Joseph — a relentless adventure seeker with a surprise in store for his friends? Recall a time when God seemed to be guiding you to new heights, new views, if only you would "look up." How are you struck by the image of someone meeting you on the front porch with the one thing you most need: a warm blanket?

What Bible stories or Christian practices does this story recall for you? **EXPLORE** whether this story holds an Aha! moment or points toward an action for you here. What is there about this story or the way it made you feel about yourself or God that you want to act on or continue pondering? What is there about this story and your reflection on it that helps you hear God speaking to your life today?

Take a moment to jot down answers to any of these questions and, especially, to remind yourself later of a story from your own life that this story called to mind.

What Others Experienced

There was an audible sigh of relief and relaxation at the end of Kathleen's story. Some people laughed out loud as they recalled similar stories from their own lives. A guy named Troy shared his fear that the car was going to crash and that Kathleen's story was going to end tragically. He was relieved at the happy ending. A girl named Hope said she could feel the strain and pressure of school, work, and college admissions evaporate completely as she imagined looking up at the stars.

It wasn't too long before someone mentioned how directly this story reminded them of Psalm 8:3–5. The psalm reads,

> When I look at your heavens, the work of your fingers,
>   the moon and the stars that you have established;

what are human beings that you are mindful of them,
  mortals that you care for them?
Yet you have made them a little lower than God,
  and crowned them with glory and honor.

Another connection was with the old church hymn
"How Great Thou Art." In language that sounds old-
fashioned today, the hymn says,

O Lord my God! when I in awesome wonder
Consider all the worlds thy hands have made,
I see the stars, I hear the rolling thunder,
Thy power throughout the universe displayed;
Then sings my soul, my savior God to Thee,
How great thou art, how great thou art!
—*Presbyterian Hymnal,* #467

THE SPIRITUAL PRACTICE OF EXAMEN

There's a way in which Kathleen's story mirrors the Ignatian spiritual practice known as examen, described simply in the book *Sleeping with Bread* by Dennis, Sheila, and Matthew Linn (Mahwah, NJ: Paulist Press, 1995). Examen is a process of ending the day by lighting a candle, becoming aware of God's loving presence, and taking about five minutes of quiet to ask two questions: "For what moment today am I *most* grateful? For what moment today am I *least* grateful?" Kathleen begins the story by telling about the extreme pressure she was feeling. She ends it by expressing the miracle of beholding God's creation and her part in it. You can learn more about the practice of examen (which may sound a lot like the "highs and lows" you might have shared at youth group) at http://www.upperroom.org/methodx/thelife/prayermethods/examen.asp.

A guy named Carson named an Aha! moment. "This story will always remind me of the importance of keeping life in perspective," he said. "It's like an alarm that goes off, reminding me to look up at the stars when I feel the pressure kicking in." Someone else named an action to which the story pointed: "We can all be Joseph every now and then, can't we? I mean we can be that person who provides a moment of Sabbath for a friend. What's stopping us?"

DAY NINE

My Mom's Room

By Melanie, age seventeen, recalling a memory from her middle school years

Every step down those stairs was making me more and more afraid of what condition my mom would be in this morning. It had been a long night, possibly the longest of my life. Mom's breathing had become very heavy. She didn't even have the strength to clear her throat. It was terrifying sitting there not being able to do anything.

At some point during the night, she told my dad to call her parents, and we all knew why. I thought, "This is it. . . . She doesn't have much more time." When they arrived, the looks on their faces expressed how I was feeling. I suddenly remembered having gone to the funeral home earlier that day and felt a rush of relief that all the planning was done.

I remember a very strong taste of fear. I was expecting the worst. I couldn't think straight. It took all my energy just to remember to breathe. It was like I was already in the fog you hear people talk about after someone passes away. It was like nothing I had ever experienced before, watching my mom struggle just to breathe.

I stood there in shock watching her fight with everything she had, not knowing what to do. I had to leave periodically for fear of breaking down and also just to take a breath of air. It felt like I was suffocating.

As I walk down the steps now, the next morning, I don't recall many details from the night before, other than intense fear, a heavy cloak of worry, and extreme sadness. It's all a blur to me now. At some point, my three siblings and I had fallen asleep in the living room in the very early hours of the morning. I don't even remember going up to my room that night, but I got there somehow, because now I am walking down the stairs in the wee hours of the morning to check on her.

I don't know what to expect. I'm numb. I hear a strange sound: silence. That means the oxygen is off. I'm thinking that it is all over, that I have lost the most important thing in my life. I somehow get up the courage to open the door. To my utter amazement, Mom is sitting up in her bed smiling and ready to greet me.

I don't know what to feel: whether to feel elated, relieved, sad that last night even happened, or afraid that this moment is too good to be true. I know it's real though, because it is like no other feeling that I have ever experienced before.

She is so alert. It is amazing. Her breathing is as if nothing had ever been wrong. There in the wee morning hours, sitting up in her bed, Mom wants to talk to me! She wants to know what is going on in my life. It has been so long since she was able to do that with me. I take advantage of it. She asks me all kinds of questions, and I am so glad she is here to talk to.

It's like she has been gone, maybe on a trip or something, and is just coming back and wants to know everything that's going on. While we're talking, I just can't help thinking to myself that she is amazing, and it just proves to me every day how miraculous her life is.

On this morning, it's like I'm in another time and place. It's as though the night before had never happened. It's as though that was just a bad dream, and I woke up, and it all went away. Deep down, I do know last night happened and that the end will come soon, but I feel like hiding from reality just for a little while, here in the comfort of my mom's room.

Practice L.I.V.E.

After you've read Melanie's story, take a deep breath and close your eyes for a moment or two. **LISTEN** to the responses it calls forth in you. If you've ever experienced the loss of a loved one, this story may hit you harder than most stories in this book. Don't be afraid of those emotions. Just allow yourself to sit with the story, and **IMMERSE** yourself in the feelings that bubble up in you.

What feelings can you name? Did your body tense during part of the story and relax at another? Did you find yourself breathing differently or beginning to feel like crying? Sometimes stories like Melanie's bring forth heaviness or a tight feeling in the chest. Then there are the feelings of surprise, disbelief, and amazement that come when Melanie finds her mom alert and awake. It's not the dismal fulfillment of her worst fears but a cherished moment she never dreamed was possible. What feelings do you have at this point in the story? Jot down the full range of feelings the story raised in you, from beginning to end. Of what stories from your own life did this story remind you? With whom or what in the story did you identify?

After you've sat for a few minutes with those feelings, **VIEW IT WIDER.** Begin to wonder where God is in the story. Where is God in the heaviness and fear around the death of a loved one? Where is God in the gift of one more visit, unexpected but so very special? What Bible stories or Christian practices does this story recall for you?

After sitting for a while with the first three steps, move on to **EXPLORE** what this story might be calling you to do or be. Is there an Aha! moment for you here? What is there about this story or the way it made you feel about yourself or God that you want to continue pondering? Is there something about this story and your reflection on it that helps you hear God speaking to your life today? Is there an action toward which it points?

Take a moment to jot down answers to any of these questions and, especially, to remind yourself later of a story from your own life that this story called to mind.

What Others Experienced

Encircled by her friends, Melanie wept at the end of this story. Her mom died of pancreatic cancer a few weeks after the day Melanie recalls here. After a time of crying and comforting, Melanie and her friends began to talk about the story—which had happened a year earlier. Melanie had since been under the good care of a grief counselor.

After a flurry of Kleenex and nose blowing, the friends began to talk in gentle whispers. They named God's presence in this momentary gift of life and love in the midst of a long, slow sadness.

Our lives are like fifth Gospels, writes a woman named Judith Siqueira. "Each of us is the pen with which God is writing a fifth gospel" (*In God's Image* 13, no. 4 [Winter, 1994]: 2-4). Matthew, Mark, Luke, and John are the four Gospels passed down through time that reflect God's direct revelation to us through the person of Jesus Christ.

But there are moments in our own lives when God continues to reveal God's self to us—often in the form of a loving, compassionate community.

In the moments following Melanie's story, her friends were the pens with which God wrote a fifth Gospel, there in that room, as the story was told, heard, held, and honored. We didn't get very far into *naming* the presence of God that day; we just sat there in it.

Later, as I reflected on Melanie's story with a different group, a strong theme emerged. In many ways, life teaches us to move on quickly from our deep sorrow. This story is about sitting with the pain long enough to feel it truly. When we trust ourselves to grieve fully, we are honoring our loss. We can sometimes hear God's still, small voice telling us that even though a loss *feels* unsurvivable, we *can* move through it. Trying to hold back grief is like trying to hold back the waves of the ocean. We can spend an incredible amount of energy attempting to avoid grief, but the energy is wasted. Grief will find a way to move through us: why not lovingly embrace it?

Emma said it reminded her of the song "Stand in the Rain" recorded by the band Superchick, which she and her friends proceeded to belt out together: "So stand in the rain. Stand your ground. . . . stand through the pain. You won't drown" (*Beauty from Pain*, 2006). Emma reflected on the connection between the song and Melanie's story. "The rain is the tears. If you keep it all inside it will find a way out. If you hold it in too long, it'll be like a flood."

For Emma, God was in Melanie's tears, but God was also in the moment she walked downstairs instead of going back to sleep. "God was the urge in her saying go, go, go," Emma stated passionately. Allison said the story called forth an action in her. "It makes me want to go to a friend who's going through a hard time and be those comforting arms," she said. "I will be her shoulder to cry on. I will be there for her."

Are you the kind of person who can help a friend walk through a deep loss, be it of a loved one, a relationship, or a heartfelt hope for the future? This is a special gift. How can you nurture it?

DAY TEN

Find a Story

Think of a friend who you know has a story to tell. It may be a story that has occurred to you during your daily meditation on these stories. Perhaps it's a friend who has told you about a significant dream or an experience that occurred on a mission trip. Maybe it's someone who's been sharing with you her journey of grief after the loss of a loved one. Maybe it's a parent or grandparent with a story you only vaguely remember but are curious about now.

Go ask that person to tell it. Write it below.

LISTEN to the story, then ask the storyteller to **IMMERSE** in the feelings the telling brings up.

Together **VIEW IT WIDER.** Where do you each see God in the story? Does it remind you of any stories you learned from the Bible as a kid or last week? Does it have a direct connection to a Christian practice, such as feeding the hungry or healing the sick? **EXPLORE** any action this story and your reflection on it call forth in you. Did you experience any Aha! moments you'd like to remember?

DAY ELEVEN

No Swimming

By Derrick, age twenty-eight, reflecting on a high-school memory

The campus of the retreat center shared space with several farmers. There was a large main building at the bottom of the slope, where our cabins were sprinkled amidst grassy areas on which cows grazed. On the second day my friends insisted that I go swimming with them. I had yet to tell them I couldn't swim. As creative as my mind was, I couldn't come up with anything that would keep me out of the pool and allow me to save face. I planned to simply sit on the side and put my feet in the water.

I had not brought swimming trunks with me, so there I was, in rather thin shorts with no underwear, walking the gravel road toward the pool. It would've been shorter to cross over the grassy areas, but the cows had left gifts that we wanted to avoid.

I made my way to the pool and sat, according to plan. A girl named Jill, who I had met earlier, immediately came my way.

"Why don't you come in the pool?" Jill asked.

"Well, I just don't feel like it." I replied, not even convincing myself. She regarded me a moment and simply said, "You can't swim, can you?"

"No, I can't," I said, not even wanting to pretend or protest.

"Well, I'll teach you. Come on." With this, Jill started to encourage me with her hands on my back.

"No, I really don't want to today," I said, resisting a little.

"Come on, it's not hard," she said, starting to push me. I struggled against her and started to push away. Some other friends came to her aid. As they all tried to get me in the water I pushed with Herculean effort and was winning. Jill gripped the back of my shorts and pulled up. The stress was simply too great for the crotch seam, which suddenly split.

I fell with a splat on the slightly wet surface of the poolside and sat there, stunned, my shorts now wrapped around my torso, my arms in the air, and my nude body sitting exposed before them.

Of course, Jill was mortified. As I hurriedly pulled down the shorts (now more like a skirt) and got up to leave, I could hear Jill saying with earnestness, "I'm so sorry. Oh my God, I'm so sorry."

That mattered to me, but it changed little about how I was feeling: humiliated, incredulous, and desperate. I made my way to the locker room to think. All I could do was go back to the cabin.

I left the building running, not thinking, through the grass, jumping over the cow patties as I flew. At one point, I strained forward, jumped over a cow patty, and slipped forward as my feet touched the grass. The momentum was enough to flatten me on my stomach, slide me forward, and finish the job on my shorts. Naked, I ran the remaining fifteen yards. Once inside, I went straight to my room.

I stayed in the cabin, a recluse, for the rest of the day. Around suppertime my desire for food overcame my fear of facing the crowd. So I made my way to the main building, late. As I entered the hall, I could feel the eyes and hear in my mind the conversations that suddenly turned to me. I saw my friends and walked to them. Without words, they slid apart to make room for me on the picnic bench. As I sat down, one of them said to me, "Derrick, if you wanted to learn how to swim, all you had to do was ask." I knew supper would be just fine.

Practice L.I.V.E.

After you've read Derrick's story, take a deep breath, and close your eyes for a moment or two. **LISTEN** to the responses it calls forth in you.

Now **IMMERSE** yourself in the feelings. Share them if you are in a group. Can you imagine the camp or smell the chlorine of the pool? Did you see the awkward moment coming and tense your body? Recall a time in your life when you wished you could just disappear. With whom or what in the story did you identify? Note the full range of emotions you feel when you listen to this story or when you remember yourself in a bathing suit in front of your peers as your body began to mature.

After you've sat for a few minutes with those feelings, begin to **VIEW IT WIDER.** Wonder where God is in the story. Is there a story from Scripture that seems to speak to you? Where is God when we get pushed into a pool in which we're not prepared to swim? Is God in the refuge, the empty cabin where Derrick hides? Or is God in the moment he musters the courage to face the crowd? Is God the community that silently slides apart, making room for Derrick and his deflated self? What's a biblical word or phrase for the knowledge that everything will be just fine?

Now is the time to **EXPLORE** future actions to which this story might be pointing. Ask yourself if there is an Aha! moment for you here. What in this story or the way it made you feel about yourself or God do you want to continue pondering? What is there about this story and your reflection on it that helps you hear God speaking to your life today? Take a moment to jot down answers to any of these questions and, especially, to remind yourself later of a story from your own life that this story called to mind.

What Others Experienced

It was as if everyone in the circle had experienced Derrick's story. We had all had that feeling in the pit of our stomachs—the one you get when you dream you showed up at school in your pajamas or, worse, realize you are nude in front of a room full of people. Feelings of humiliation, embarrassment, and shame resonated with us all. Kevin named loneliness. The cabin after Derrick's sudden retreat seemed like one of the loneliest places on earth. But there was also shared relief at the moment Derrick's friends saw him enter the cafeteria and slid over to open a space for him.

As we reflected on this story, we thought of womanist theologians who write about how God is well known for making "a way out of no way" for African Americans. Historically speaking, this phrase refers to slaves on the Atlantic passage, whose survival on the journey itself showed God making "a way out of no way." It also refers to conditions under slavery in the South, and the resilience of a people who secretly sang escape routes into their spirituals and hung messages of warning and sanctuary on the quilts airing in the sunshine. The Underground Railroad was a "way out of no way."

WHAT IS A WOMANIST?

Womanist is a word coined by novelist Alice Walker in the book *In Search of Our Mother's Gardens* (San Francisco: Harcourt Brace Jovanovich, 1983). It became a term used to describe the writings of women in church and the academy who name the importance of their identity as black women while also claiming connection with feminism and with the African American community, male and female. The concept creates space for women to claim their roots in black history, religion, and culture. For more information about womanism, its history, and its theological method, go to www.religion-online.org/showarticle.asp?title=445 or check out Katie Geneva Canon's book *Katie's Canon: Womanism and the Soul of the Black Community* (New York: Continuum, 1995) and Delores Williams's *Sisters in the Wilderness* (New York: Maryknoll, NY: Orbis, 1983).

Derrick, who is African American, resonated with this idea. In his utter humiliation and embarrassment, Derrick fled to the only safe space he knew. Hunger drew him out, and his friends helped carve a path of reentry. It felt like a "way out of no way."

This story also reminded folks of the ways in which Jesus always seemed to include others: the woman accused of adultery, the lepers, and the tax collectors. Whoever seemed to be on the "outside" strangely ended up on the "inside" in the stories of Jesus. This led Neil to name his Aha! moment. "We're called to slide over and let the 'outcast' in, whether it's Derrick after losing his shorts or someone even more difficult to accept," Neil said. "I think this story will remind me that if I say I am following the path of Jesus, I had better always practice inclusion."

How are you like one of Derrick's friends, alert to the one who may be in pain, seeking ways to work with God to carve a "way out of no way"?

DAY TWELVE

"Hakuna Shida"

By Adella, age nineteen, telling a story from the previous summer

"Hey, Auntie!"

The sound of his voice greets me through the Tanzanian summer air. Michael's joy is pure, and it is alive every day without fail. He sprints toward me, bounding with an energy and natural rhythm I imagine only wild animals possess. He is grinning brighter than sunshine; he is beaming—a spirit, wrapped in beautiful, dark skin, reaching out into the world.

"Habari za leo mpenzi?" ("How are you today my love?")

"Nzuri auntie! Sasa njoo hapa!" ("Very good! Now come here!")

I skip over to greet him with an enormous hug. He wants to run around back to the swings, which are simply large ropes dangling off the trees. I would love to scamper away with him and revel in our new friendship, but I can't. I tell him that today is going to be different. Today I am not a playmate. I have to sit in the office; Mama Margaret wants me to do some work. He reacts to the news as expected. His emotion is always uninhibited, blatant. His brow furrows, and his mouth forms into an overdone and melodramatic grimace to show his disappointment.

"Youuuu noooo fuuuuhhhhn!"

Then he bursts into laughter, which seems to spill out of the center of him. He smiles at me with his eyes and runs off into the yard, sweeping his younger brother up into his arms and away behind the trees.

I feel my stomach tighten and my nerves begin to race. He is right. Today is not going to be fun. Today I am here to record the children's stories one by one. I am here to listen to them share why they are living at the orphanage. I already know most of the stories; Margaret has shared them with me to help me understand certain behaviors. But what we know is the bare facts, told from the perspective of the adults who brought them here. We don't know what the children understand, what they feel, what they live. I ask if we can talk to Michael first, to get the hardest out of the way. Over the past two months, Michael and I have grown very close. He is my dearest friend here.

He comes in, and I can tell that Margaret has told him what we are doing by the way he is carrying himself. The excited, bounding leaps have stopped. The look in his eye suggests that he has already become saddened before the words have even come out. He wants to look up at me, but he has to fight to do so. He sits beside me.

Ibrah is in the room with us to help translate. I won't be able to understand most of what Michael is saying. My Swahili is limited to encouraging, childlike conversational phrases. I haven't yet learned the language for trauma.

Michael, who is now eleven, lost his parents two years ago. Upon finding out that they were both HIV-positive, his father beat his mother to death with a wooden plank. Michael and his younger brother, Lorenti, were in the room and watched this happen. As Michael understands it, his father did not like that they were sick. It made him angry, so he lashed out. Michael says he was confused at how angry his father was. He was terrified by the violence. I was looking at my fingers type out each word, glancing up to look at his face. I was thinking, over and over, "How could this child have witnessed all of this?" After the beating, their father left the house and disappeared. Michael found him in the woods nine days later. He had shot himself. Michael said he screamed at his father that he needed him to wake up. Then he realized that he was dead.

He says that he sees his mother in his dreams. He says that he cannot eat when he thinks about her. He says he does not know how to forget her face, how to forget her holding him. Now he is crying. His shoulders are bent over, tears and snot slowly drip down his face. He is heaving. The sound coming out of this little boy is the worst thing I have ever heard. It is the sound of torment and panic and fury. The sound beats violently inside of me. It is the sound of something made to be whole and pure shattering and slapping itself on the ground. This is his cry.

There is a flickering knowledge in me that pain and suffering is something that every human must bear, but to hear its initial grievance come in this piercing and absolute way makes my own heart break, as if I had forgotten that pain existed and suddenly remembered it again. I wake up to the nature of death anew.

What do I do? How do I love him? I don't know. I wrap my arms around him and bring his head close to me. He gasps a few more deep breaths, releases a few more whimpers, and then the cadence of his crying and swaying frame slow and come to a hush, a rest.

I wipe the last tear. He sighs. Then he looks up at me, and a smile breaks out. There is power in the upturned corners of his mouth. His smile cuts through the thick and unbreathable air that had been filling the room. Now the air is giving us life again. His joy has resurfaced. We can breathe.

"Haya haya, Auntie. *Kesho, tucheze, Tafadhali."* ("Okay, Auntie. Tomorrow we have to play. Please.")

"Ndio kwa kweli mpenzi." ("Yes, of course, my love.")

The unconquerable spirit is again pulsing through the young boy.

He looks at me, starts to walk away, and then looks back. Our eyes meet, and they speak for us. He sees the sorrow I am feeling for him, and he doesn't want me to feel it, so he laughs.

"Hakuna shida, Auntie!" ("It is no worry, Auntie.")

Then he skips out of the room in one fluid rush of joy and runs away to retrieve his brother.

Practice L.I.V.E.

After you've **LISTENED** to Adella's story, take a deep breath. Allow yourself to be fully present to the responses it calls forth in you. Now **IMMERSE** yourself in the feelings that arise. With whom in the story do you identify? Does it remind you of any stories from your own life?

After you've sat for a few minutes with those feelings, begin to **VIEW IT WIDER.** Wonder where God is in the story. Is there a story from Scripture that seems to speak to you with reference to Adella's story? Where is God in the face of great suffering? Or in the suffering of an innocent child?

After sitting for a while with the first three steps, ask yourself if there is a potential action to **EXPLORE.** What is there about this story or the way it made you feel about yourself or God that you might want to act on?

What is there about this story and your reflection on it that helps you hear God speaking to your life today? Take a moment to jot down answers to any of these questions and, especially, to remind yourself later of a story from your own life that this story called to mind.

What Others Experienced

Adella and two close friends sat in a cozy corner of a college-town tearoom as we did L.I.V.E. with this story. We were curled up on pillows, leisurely drinking chai until she began to read her story. Then we fell silent, set down our teacups, and focused entirely on her. The story descended on all of us, and at the end we were feeling very connected to her pain.

The facts we all know about AIDS in Africa and the epidemic of orphans registered anew in us through Michael's story. We expressed how utterly desolate it made us feel, especially in the description of the murder of Michael's mom, the suicide of his dad, and the aloneness that resulted for the children. Adella's description of Michael reminded Rebecca of children she had met on a mission trip to the Dominican Republic.

At first, we didn't want to go looking for God in this story. We didn't want to move too quickly to Michael's eyes looking back to check on Adella, and the joy that returned as quickly as it had departed. We wanted to allow ourselves a long moment just to feel the pain of the world.

"Your heart was broken open," Lisbeth said. We talked about how in moments of brokenheartedness we are very near to the heart of God. Adella named an Aha! moment: "I know that if I want to get closer to God, I must go to where there is brokenheartedness in the world."

For Adella, God was present in the moment in which she and Michael comforted and held one another, but God was *most* present in the return of joy. "God for me is in the very end of the story where Michael looks back at me and laughs. That was like God talking to me."

WHAT IS THE CATHOLIC WORKER MOVEMENT?

Founded by activist Dorothy Day in the 1930s, the Catholic Worker Movement is grounded in a belief in the God-given dignity of every person. It is committed to nonviolence, voluntary poverty, prayer, and hospitality to the homeless, hungry, and forsaken. Over 185 Catholic Worker communities exist around the world. You can learn more about them from www.catholicworker.org or by reading Dorothy Day's biography *A Long Loneliness* (New York: Harper Collins, 1952), which tells the story of her search for community in confronting the world's evil and injustice. Today, movements such as The School for New Monasticism establish micro-communities of action and prayer in much the same way as Catholic Worker Houses. Check them out at http://www.newmonasticism.org/people.php.

I asked her to say more about this. She added, "It was just like the disciples going to the tomb on Easter morning. I expected to find death, but I found new life. To me, God is in Michael's joy. That's the Easter story retold before my eyes."

Rebecca said the story reminded her of something a roommate had recently told her. Rebecca had just returned from a Catholic Worker House, a community center where college students and homeless people work side by side to prepare meals and share them. After a few months of hanging out there, Rebecca found that she no longer wondered who was a student and who was homeless. She trained her brain not to ask that question and became comfortable. One night, as she told her roommate about a man she had worked with and the gentle hug he offered at the end of the evening, her roommate said, "You just hugged Jesus." Rebecca said she thinks of this almost daily, wondering to herself, "When am I going to hug Jesus today?"

DAY THIRTEEN

Let It Out

By Debra, age thirty-six, telling a story from her adolescence

Secret dreams. We all have them. When I was a teenager,
my dream was Broadway. Many young girls dream of
being on stage. When I was in high school, most of the girls
I knew who dreamed of Broadway pictured themselves as
Annie. Musical revues of Annie were performed in schools
across America in the late 1970s, and nearly every girl who
dreamed of Broadway could sing "Tomorrow" in her sleep.
Except for me. When I dreamed, I sang different songs.

The problem with dreams is that so often they slip away
with the morning light. The sad truth is that there is only
one Annie, and most of us end up as orphans in the chorus
if we want to be on stage. I was, unfortunately, a perfect
choice to play the part of an orphan. I was quiet, short,
tiny, and demure, and I preferred lurking in the shadows
to stepping into the spotlight. I loved singing, but I sang
in a whispered voice, afraid of what others would think
if they heard the sounds coming from within me. I never
sang loudly; I never auditioned for solos; and I always hid,
sitting in the back row during class.

It's impossible to know what prompted Mrs. Jones to ask me to stay after the bell rang. My heart pounded with fear, and my mind raced with possibilities, wondering what I could possibly have done to result in this summons.

While I don't recall the exact words, the reason for the summons shook me to the core. I was still terrified, though not because I was in trouble. It was much worse than being in trouble. Mrs. Jones wanted me to sing one of the roles in the show. And she didn't want me to sing just any role. She wanted me to sing the one role nobody else wanted. She wanted me to sing the only role I dreamed about singing: Miss Hannigan. Mrs. Jones wanted me to sing the part of the old, crotchety, cruel, drunken spinster. My dream role!

As is often the case when turning dreams into reality, there were, of course, problems. While I am certainly not tiny or shy now, I was both as a teenager. I practiced privately after school with Mrs. Jones for the better part of three weeks. When the time came for me to sing for the first time in rehearsal, I opened my mouth and squeaked. As any singer can tell you, fear is not such a good thing for the voice. Mrs. Jones stopped playing, comforted me with a smile, and quietly commanded, "Close your eyes and sing." Dutifully, I closed my eyes, took a deep breath, and let my voice spill out from that space in which I kept it locked away. The first thing I noticed was the silence. I opened my eyes to the stunned stares of classmates. After what seemed like days but was surely only mere seconds, I heard raucous cheering and applause.

On opening night, I stepped forward and smiled as I spotted my family in the audience. The response of the other choir members had given me confidence, and I was looking forward to surprising my family. I will never forget the stunned looks on their faces, nor my enjoyment of their surprise.

With occasional hiatuses, I continue to dabble in the performing arts, and it is always a joy when I witness the pleasure it brings to people's lives, including the lives of my family and friends. I am no longer the quiet, tiny, frightened girl hiding in the back row. Thanks to Mrs. Jones, my classmates, my friends, and my family, I found my voice and learned to give thanks and enjoy it as the gift it is.

To this day, I have no idea what prompted Mrs. Jones's decision. However, I do remember one thing she said when she asked me to sing the role: "I know you can do this. I know you've got this inside you. Just close your eyes, take a deep breath, and let it out."

Practice L.I.V.E.

After you've read Debra's story, take a deep breath. **LIS-TEN** to the responses it calls forth in you. Now **IMMERSE** yourself in the feelings the story evokes. Recall your feelings and associations. With whom did you identify in the story?

After you've sat for a few minutes with those feelings, begin to **VIEW IT WIDER**. Wonder where God is in the story. How has God spoken through music and song in your life? Who helped you discover your voice, whether spoken, written, sung, or through some other outlet?

After sitting for a while with the first three steps, ask yourself if there is an Aha! moment for you here. **EXPLORE** any actions that this story might be calling forth in you.

What is there about this story and your reflection on it that helps you hear God speaking to your life today? Take a moment to jot down answers to any of these questions and, especially, to remind yourself later of a story from your own life that this story called to mind.

What Others Experienced

When Debra looked up after reading this story, she was greeted by the faces of her classmates: twenty-two women and one man who were taking time away from work as Christian educators and youth ministers to complete their master's degrees. Debra and her classmates had shared many meals together and knew well many of the intricacies of one another's personalities, jobs, and family situations. When Debra's story ended, there were smiles and a few tears. People were quick to begin sharing their feelings, captured in such comments as "I am celebrating with you!" and "I feel like I was in the audience!" The joy was almost palpable. Several people shared memories of significant teachers, pastors, or mentors who had noticed a gift and urged it into blossoming. Debra's story brought to my mind a home economics teacher who had asked me to give the devotion at a state convention of the Future Homemakers of America when I was in the ninth grade. Mrs. Doak believed in me and was able to see a gift I could only barely imagine.

After I shared this memory, gentle laughter erupted as other women shared similar memories. We talked about how many of these moments marked the beginning of our young selves discovering a gift for speaking, singing, or otherwise "finding voice." Feminist scholar Nelle Morton calls this "being heard into speech" (*The Journey Is Home* [Boston: Beacon Press, 1985]). We noted how Debra was "heard into speech" by Mrs. Jones. In telling the story, Debra was naming an important part of her vocational journey.

The conversation turned toward some of the common experiences shared by women who experience a call to ministry. Ministry is a profession traditionally held by men and one that many women could not imagine themselves

GIRLFRIEND THEOLOGY

Girls' inner voices are sometimes hidden by our culture's expectations about how girls and women are supposed to act, be, or behave. I wrote *Doing Girlfriend Theology: God-Talk with Young Women* (Cleveland: Pilgrim Press, 2005) to help girls connect with their inner voices and to foster connection between girls and women. Girlfriend theology—which uses the same four steps as L.I.V.E.—is one way that adult women can be part of "hearing into speech" the voices and stories of younger women. This is particularly important in a world in which girls are still often told that their worth can be measured by their sexiness, thinness, or consumption of products marketed to them. To help you think about the lives of contemporary adolescent girls, watch Rachel Simmon's PBS video *A Girl's Life* at http://video.pbs.org/video/1367248470/ or listen to the lyrics of "The Fear," a song by Lily Allen, at http://www.youtube.com/watch?v=qn7ziS43YHs&feature=youtube_gdata. For a moving tribute to the global movement of educating girls, see www.girleffect.com.

stepping into only a generation ago. The struggle to name one's gifts when they don't come in a socially acceptable package was a common memory for many of us.

When we turned to looking for God in the story, Tammy said that God was working through Mrs. Jones to bring Debra out of hiding and to give her the confidence she would need to begin expressing her gift to the world. Others immediately began to name times when Jesus pointed to the presence, significance, or worth of women. Like Mrs. Jones, Jesus had a way of noticing things that might easily have been overlooked or deemed unimportant. Stories of Mary and Martha, the story of the woman healed of a flow of blood, and the importance of Miriam in the Old Testament and Lydia in the New Testament all flooded into the conversation. We thought of Shiprah and Puah, the midwives who saved Moses. We thought of Ruth and Naomi, forging a friendship of familial significance in spite of patriarchal social norms. The conversation grew solemn as Ann exclaimed, "I'm so glad these stories were left *in*!" Her Aha! moment involved taking in, not for the first time but at a renewed level, the importance of women's stories in the biblical witness. Remembering these often-unnamed women has been an important task to scholars who have helped pave a way for women over the last fifty years to claim roles of leadership in contemporary faith communities.

DAY FOURTEEN

The Kiss

By Andrew, age twenty-nine, recalling a story from when he was in high school

I have a confession. When I was in high school, I was a band geek. I played tuba in marching band, concert band, and orchestra. As a result, I got to go on a lot of cool trips. My freshman and junior years, the marching band went to Disney World. My sophomore year, the concert band and orchestra went to Virginia Beach and Busch Gardens, which is a big trip when you're coming from Massachusetts. Our senior band trip, however, was to Six Flags New England. In retrospect, I was very lucky to be in a band program that took trips every year. At the time, though, I was expecting a weeklong trip to a real tourist destination, and instead I got a day trip to a local theme park most people haven't heard of. I was mad.

However, something happened that made that trip pretty awesome. There was this girl named Samantha, and I had developed a crush on her in seventh grade that never really went away. Sure, I had dated some girls in high school, but I had never liked them as much as I liked Samantha. So,

I was hanging out at Six Flags with Samantha and some other friends. I don't know what her motivation was—it might have been end-of-high-school euphoria, or maybe she was just being a seventeen-year-old girl—but she was flirting with me.

Samantha had this stupid plastic wand that she had won at one of the carnival games there (you know how cheap carnival game prizes are). She told me to close my eyes and make a wish and she would wave the wand and make it come true. I was thinking, "Well, that's pretty stupid, but she's pretty, so I'll do it." I don't remember what I wished for, but I'm sure it had something to do with going out with Samantha. When I opened my eyes, she kissed me on the cheek. It was just a peck, and nothing ever came of it, but that kiss is one of my fondest high school memories. In the end, it was a pretty good day.

Practice L.I.V.E.

After you've read Andrew's story, take a deep breath. Close your eyes, and welcome the feelings that wash over you. **LISTEN** to the responses it calls forth in you. Now **IMMERSE** yourself in the feelings that arise. With whom in the story do you identify? Does it remind you of a particular time in your life?

After you've sat for a few minutes with those feelings and shared them if you are in a group, begin to **VIEW IT WIDER.** Wonder where God is in the story. Is there a story from Scripture that seems somehow connected? Is there an image of God that bubbles up?

After sitting for a while with the **LISTENING, IMMERSING,** and **VIEWING IT WIDER,** ask yourself where there is an Aha! moment for you here. **EXPLORE** if there is an action to which this story might be calling you.

What is there about this story or the way it made you feel about yourself or God that you want to continue pondering? What is there about this story and your reflection on it that helps you hear God speaking to your life today? Take a moment to jot down answers to any of these questions and, especially, to remind yourself later of a story from your own life that this story called to mind.

What Others Experienced

We were all smiling at the end of Andrew's story, in part because he was a little embarrassed to tell it, even now, almost a decade later. We could all "feel him" in that! We shared our feelings associated with adolescent awkwardness, the thrill of attraction, flirtation, embarrassment, and wistfulness. Martin said the story reminded him of times when he "should have kissed, but didn't." Joanne said she felt solidarity: "I, too, was a band geek. I got my first kiss on a band trip." Everyone shared stories of their first kiss. One woman, who was surprised by a kiss from a much-admired guy said, "I kind of walked a little different after that."

As we moved on to think about God and Scripture, the first biblical references to kisses that came to mind were about betrayal, which didn't seem to fit here. Then we remembered the Song of Solomon, the only book in the Bible expressly about romantic love and human desire. We wondered, with a bit of humor, why that book is so seldom preached or taught. We wondered if people might have a less distorted view of sensuality, sexuality, and romantic love if it came wrapped in understandings of God's created beauty more often. Andrew's story about a seventh-grade crush and a long-wished-for kiss seems nicely echoed in the verse "I am my beloved's, and his desire is for me" (Song

7:10). We talked about how human sexuality, although often avoided in Christian education, can be an important part of our spiritual journey. The dawning ability to desire another person awakens the capacity to see oneself as desirable, as lovable, as wanted beyond all others.

The talk then turned toward being "chosen." Out of all the people on the trip with whom Samantha could have flirted, she chose Andrew. God is in that moment when we are seen for our own special gifts, when we're called out and chosen. We talked about the biblical story of David's brothers being overlooked in the lineup, but we couldn't

---

REMEMBER THE CONCORDANCE?

This story, with its emphasis on a kiss and its hint toward sexuality, is a great place to turn to a concordance. Do a quick search of words having to do with human sexuality, such as *kiss, body, sex, marriage, family,* and *love.* You'll see an immense variety of ways in which marriage and sexuality get expressed in God's story through the ancient Hebrews. It's interesting that Jesus forgives an adulterer, yet we never hear him talk on many topics church folk fight a lot about, such as homosexuality. Although some people say there is one "biblical view" on sexuality, it is striking to find that the Bible actually says very many different things about it. This doesn't mean that the Bible is inconsistent; rather it points to the fact that the Bible is a compilation of stories coming out of vastly different contexts. Weighing the stories that help give our lives meaning and direction is a primary reason methods like L.I.V.E. can be helpful. We don't have to take the easy answers, and we don't have to figure out the complexities alone. A concordance is a handy tool to have nearby when doing L.I.V.E. with a group of people, especially if the group is not particularly familiar with Scripture. Strong's Concordance, an online tool used by biblical scholars and laypeople alike, is found at www.eliyah.com/lexicon.html.

remember it exactly. Where does that story occur in the Bible? We looked it up in the concordance and found it in 1 Samuel 16. God helped Samuel choose David, young and scrawny but mysteriously "just right" in God's eyes. Andrew read this part out loud: God "does not see as mortals see; they look on the outward appearance, but the LORD looks on the heart" (1 Sam. 16:7).

Andrew ended our time together by sharing this Aha! moment: "It felt very good to share this story. It felt good to remember how vulnerable I felt in that moment and to open myself in new ways to being vulnerable today. There's something alive in us when we are vulnerable."

Ben said this: "In the story it was a wish that got answered in a delightful surprise. In faith, it's our prayers. One day, we open our eyes, and there it is."

Allen, a youth minister, named another action: "Because of this story, I'll be more able to share my love. I want to act in this way: helping the young people I know to see how particularly they are chosen, how God is saying, 'I choose you.'"

DAY FIFTEEN

The Quilting Circle

*By Brenda, age forty-five, remembering a story from her
teenage years*

I blinked my eyes rapidly as I welcomed the sunshine
streaming in through my window. The wintry morning
air was pungent with the smell of Maxwell House coffee,
country ham, and freshly applied Old English furniture
polish. As I tried to bury myself deeper into the warm ruts
of the comfortable feather bed that had been my sick bed
for the last three days, I remembered that this was the day
that my grandmother and her friends would begin their
annual three-day quilting bee.

Curious about the quilting bee, I convinced my grandmother that I was well enough and mature enough at twelve
years of age to get out of bed and join the quilting-bee ladies
with my book and pillow. Before everyone arrived, she told
me that she expected me to be on my best behavior. "Good
little girls," she said, "are to be seen and not heard."

The ladies arrived around eight o'clock that morning laden with all types of food for their lunch, including
pound cake, chicken salad, sliced ham, and potato salad. I

found it very peaceful sitting quietly and observing them as they began the process of preparing the quilt. They all sat around the loom with needle and thread in hand and began to glide their needles slowly in and out of the quilt top with tiny, very even stitches. Conversations ranged from selecting appropriate quilt patterns to new recipes for pound cake found in the Almanac.

As the afternoon wore on, the ladies' conversation turned to discussions about their individual faith journeys. This discussion led them into talking about the hardships of black people living in America, the civil rights movement, and Dr. Martin Luther King. They questioned the role of the church in the civil rights movement and commented on the need to stay in constant prayer. The room seemed to vibrate with tension as the women described their fears for their families as our community began the process of integration. There were whispered talks of the Klan visiting Sister Butler's father-in-law's house. Although the ladies agreed that integration was upsetting, they all saw it as the means for their children and grandchildren to receive the best education possible. It was at this point that Mrs. Sampson, my grandmother's neighbor, brought me into the conversation. "Brenda, what do you plan to be when you grow up?" I replied, "A nurse." "How wonderful," one of the other ladies commented, "We are very proud of you. We know that you are doing very well in school, and in times like these, that is very important. My grandmother looked me in the eyes very pointedly and said, "We did not have the opportunity to go to school because we had to work, but you will have the opportunity to go to college." "Don't let anyone tell you that you cannot achieve, and remember to keep God with you at all times," Aunt Eloise stated emphatically. "Be a good girl, and get your education first; then look for a husband." "Amen" sounded from each of the women around the loom.

The conversation shifted back to the topic of integration, but I knew that I would never forget the importance of that lazy afternoon conversation. I felt as if I had been given a charge that I would have to carry out for the rest of my life. From that moment on, I knew that the ladies around the quilting loom would be surrounding me with their amens.

Practicing L.I.V.E.

After you've read Brenda's story, take a deep breath. Allow yourself to **LISTEN** to the responses it calls forth in you.

IMMERSE yourself in your feelings. Did a circle of elders ever surround you with this kind of care or attention? When, as a youth, did you ever get to "listen in" on the serious conversations of adults around you?

After you've sat for a few minutes with the feelings, begin to **VIEW IT WIDER** and wonder where God is in the story. Is there a story from Scripture that seems to speak to you?

After sitting for a while with the first three steps, ask yourself what actions or changes in your life this story might call you to **EXPLORE**. Is there an Aha! moment for you here? What is there about this story or the way it made you feel about yourself or God that you want to continue pondering? Is there something about this story and your reflection on it that helps you hear God speaking to your life today?

Take a moment to jot down answers to any of these questions and, especially, to remind yourself later of a story from your own life that this story called to mind.

What Others Experienced

There was a long, comfortable silence after Brenda told her story. When people started sharing their feelings, it was almost in whispers. There was a feeling of having touched holy ground. We didn't want to disturb the gentle presence of God's spirit that seemed to be in the room.

As we started talking, we focused our conversation on how God is present in the compassionate, caring, hospitable community gathered around the girl. It is a community that feeds one another, worries with one another, and empowers one another. A task as seemingly mundane as stitching a quilt is actually a powerful gathering where stories are told and lives are encouraged amid great struggle.

Anne made reference to the history of quilts and quilting bees as times when women created a kind of sacred space. In this story, the circle was drawn wide enough to let Brenda in. In that moment, it becomes a rite of passage. Brenda is let into grown-up conversations. The ladies asked questions and held open a space in which Brenda was able to discern how she might answer the call of the world's need in her life.

Someone mentioned the biblical story of Esther, who found herself perfectly prepared to represent her people "for such a time as this." Someone else mentioned the story

WHAT IS DISCERNMENT?

Discernment is an ongoing practice of listening for the voice of God, writes Mark Yaconelli in the book *Contemplative Youth Ministry: Practicing the Presence of Jesus* (Grand Rapids: Zondervan, 2006). In order to hear God's voice, we have to slow down, ask questions, and pay attention. That's what happened to Brenda on this day with her friends. Is there a circle of caring elders, like the ladies in the quilting circle, who are watching you, noticing your gifts, and wondering what you are going to do with them? At their best, churches can function that way for young people.

of a little girl who appears in 2 Kings 5 and tells a Syrian general how to find a prophet of Yahweh who will cure his leprosy. In both of these stories, communities had nurtured young women to take a role in changing the world. Brenda's story was a retelling of these old, old stories.

DAY SIXTEEN

Harlem Dream

By Adrienne, sharing a memory from high school

In the summer of 1980, I traveled to New York City intending to spend an entire week with my grandmother. She lived in Harlem around the corner from the legendary Apollo Theater. I was then an aspiring actress and dancer. I was determined not only to make it in the business but to be the first black actress to receive a Best Actress Academy Award. I had a plan. I was going to go and live with my grandmother, attend NYU to major in performing arts, and go on auditions. This trip was to be a prelude to making the dream into a reality.

My younger cousin, Tena, joined me on the trip. She was my favorite cousin and my favorite childhood friend, so her coming along just made the thought of this adventure even sweeter. My grandmother was thrilled to have me. I was her favorite, and I knew it. She didn't know Tena, who was from my father's side of my family, but she was willing to have her come if it made me happy. Grandma also supported my plan to come and live with her after graduating high school. We left for New York one Friday morning on a Trailways bus, as excited as our parents were nervous. We were on our way!

My grandmother and her girlfriend greeted us at the station. We first went to Grandma's apartment and ate lunch. We caught up on family business, and then Grandma told me of her plans for us for the entire week. She popped up these tickets she bought for all of us to go to a Broadway play. Unfortunately, both my cousin and I fell asleep during the performance.

On Saturday, we had breakfast and went shopping. My grandmother informed me that she had on her agenda for us to go to the movies with her friend's college kid. Boring. I can't even remember the movie, but I remember wanting to see something else to which my grandmother said no, stating that it wasn't age appropriate. I remember how disappointed I was. This was only day one. Part of the excitement to this trip was to be alone to do my own thing, but Grandma had her own plans.

While at the movies, my cousin and I tried to sneak away to smoke a cigarette, but we were caught. By Saturday night, my cousin was crying due to homesickness. My feeble attempts to console her failed miserably. She cried almost all night long. She was so depressed on Sunday morning that she called her mother, who talked with my mother, who talked with my grandmother. The result? My wonderful trip was cut short. By Sunday evening we were on the bus heading back to Baltimore. Both my grandmother and I were very upset. She invited me to come back again without bringing anyone else.

Practice L.I.V.E.

After you've heard Adrienne's story, take a deep breath, and **LISTEN** to the responses it calls forth in you. Now

IMMERSE yourself in the feelings this story evoked. With whom did you empathize in the story? After you've sat for a few minutes with those feelings, begin to VIEW IT WIDER. Wonder where God is in the story. Where does it intersect Scripture?

After sitting for a while with the LISTENING, IMMERSING, and VIEWING IT WIDER, ask yourself to EXPLORE any possibilities that emerge for you. Is there a way this story calls for an action or change in your life? What is there about this story or the way it made you feel about yourself or God that you want to continue pondering? Is there something about this story and your reflection on it that helps you hear God speaking to your life today?

Take a moment to jot down answers to any of these questions and, especially, to remind yourself later of a story from your own life that this story called to mind.

What Others Experienced

Some of us were deflated and feeling "absolutely sunk" at the end of this story. High hopes had been utterly dashed. "What a bummer!" said Joanne. "I feel utterly disappointed and frustrated." Others were relieved. "As the youngest of five siblings, I was always the whiner who got homesick," Andy said. "I was so glad when they got on the bus to go home." This response got resounding amens from two other men in the group who still suffer from homesickness.

As we talked about God, Gerald was quick to name it: "God is like the Grandmother. She has her plans. Clearly, her plans are different from yours." He recited Jeremiah 29:11: "For surely I know the plans I have for you, says the LORD, plans for your welfare and not for harm, to give you a future with hope." We talked about times when we wondered what plans God might have for us. Pete talked about his image of God's plan being like the broad brush-strokes of a painting to which we fill in the details. He said this fits a still-emerging understanding of God he's been reading about in process theology. "In this image of God, humans choose from many options, and God is urging us toward the best ones," Pete explained. "It's not like there's a designated plan for our lives, a way things are meant to be." Pete said that he likes this new image of God but that sometimes it conflicts with the theology he inherited, in which God is more like a computer-programmer-in-the-sky, directing humans below. "I don't ascribe to that image of God anymore," he said. "But it still creeps into my thinking every now and then."

For Cody, one who suffers homesickness, a different passage from the same chapter of Jeremiah came to mind: "Seek the welfare of the city where I have sent you into exile" (Jer. 29:7). "I often feel in exile," he said. "I've learned how to seek the welfare of this city, but part of me just wants to go home!"

As we talked about Adrienne's ruined trip and how far from fantasy the reality landed, we saw one glimmer of hope in her grandmother's invitation to visit again, alone. This, Gerald said, was God's ongoing plan, revealed to Jeremiah only when he was ready. Then Gerald took the story into the New Testament.

"It's like the disciples on Good Friday," he said. "All the expectations of Palm Sunday are dashed. They wanted an emperor king, and all they had was a dead body. But what was that he had said about three days? There's the glimmer of hope. God has a plan. Like the grandmother in the story!"

As we ended our conversation, Andy shared an Aha! moment: "This was a story about figuring out who you are and what you want to do with your gifts. In discerning vocation, the process is as important as where we end up. Moving through great disappointment into moments of knowing again . . . that's the way we roll, isn't it?"

DAY SEVENTEEN

Your Story

Who are you today?
In two or three sentences describe the way you'd introduce
yourself to a stranger today.

What's your story? Is there one that pops up for you as
you think about Andrew's kiss, Brenda's circle of caring
watchers, Debra's voice, or Adrienne's trip?

DAY EIGHTEEN

A Shocking Shade of Blue

By Kelly, age thirty-eight, remembing a day in college

I graduated from high school in the top fifteen students
in my class of four hundred, and so I was accustomed to
doing well all the things that I did. I was an officer on my
dance team. I was a medal winner on the crew team. I was
a leader of some sort in the clubs I belonged to. I had good
friends and no enemies. I started college the same way,
expecting to be successful with only moderate effort. I was
a diligent worker, bud I didn't ever have to push myself
extremely hard.

At the University of Virginia, I soon discovered thou-
sands of people whose lists of accomplishments were as
impressive as mine. Everyone had been successful in high
school—that's why they were here! By the time October
was over, I was discovering what it meant to really work
hard: There were papers to write, tons of textbooks to read,
and research to be done. I was feeling pressure to continue
getting those As as I always had before. I had broken up
with my boyfriend from home, and my best friend kept
telling me I was "too smart" to be training to be a teacher.

One day I was walking through campus, looking at the ground as I walked, trying to get straight in my head all the things I needed to get done and in what order I needed to do them. My shoulders were hunched, my forehead was furrowed, and I'm sure I was breathing short, quick breaths as I walked as fast as possible.

All of a sudden, I felt the urge to look up. When I did, I was amazed by the color of the sky—a shocking, incredible shade of blue. How did it get so blue? Then I noticed the leaves. The maple and oak trees on the lawn had the greenest leaves, and many of them were beginning to show hints of orange, yellow, and red. What colors! Then I took a deep breath, feeling the cool air rush through me, and I realized that I felt fabulous! I was alive, and I was in a beautiful place learning from an amazing assortment of talented people. My work would get done. And if it didn't, the world wouldn't end. I was able to see all the wondrous things around me. I went through the rest of the day, got done what needed to get done, and whenever I felt the stress creeping back in, I went outside, looked up, and breathed in lungs full of cool, fresh air.

Practice L.I.V.E.

After you've read Kelly's story, take a deep breath, and close your eyes for a moment or two. **LISTEN** to the responses it calls forth in you. Now **IMMERSE** yourself in the feelings. Did your body tense during part of the story and relax at another? Jot down the full range of feelings the story raised in you, from beginning to end. Of what stories from your own life did this story remind you? With whom or what in the story did you identify?

After you've sat for a few minutes with those feelings, begin to **VIEW IT WIDER.** Wonder where God is in the story. Is God "an incredible, shocking shade of blue"? Is

God in the urge to look up when the heaviness of the world is on your shoulders?

What Bible stories or Christian practices does this story recall for you? After sitting for a while **LISTEN-ING, IMMERSING,** and **VIEWING IT WIDER,** begin to **EXPLORE** what this story is asking of you. Is there an action or change you've been contemplating that is related to this story or your reflections on it? What is there about this story and your reflection on it that helps you hear God speaking to your life today?

Take a moment to jot down answers to any of these questions and, especially, to remind yourself later of a story from your own life that this story called to mind.

What Others Experienced

Markers of success start early in life, don't they? When Kelly shared this story, we talked about how some of us begin to define ourselves by our grades as early as six years of age when we start knowing about As and Bs in first

CELTIC SPIRITUALITY

Kelly's story is reminiscent of Celtic spirituality, a form of Christian tradition that originates in the British Isles and is marked with an appreciation of nature, poetry, and art. Celtic prayers and blessings overflow with the sense of creation's beauty as a gift from God. You can hear Celtic music and read Celtic prayers at this Web site: www.allsaintsbrookline .org/celtic.html. Celtic poet and author John O'Donahue reads a poem called "Blessing" that speaks to the images raised in Kelly's story at speakingoffaith.publicradio.org/programs/ john_odonahue/ss_beannacht/ss-beannacht.shtml.

There is also a poignant interview with O'Donahue at this site.

or second grade. This system can contribute to an end-less cycle of comparing ourselves to others and constantly needing to feel "ranked."

Kelly's experience of being a small fish in a big pond when she got to college felt familiar to some of us. We shared memories of juggling various classes during a busy semester. Jane remembered a recurring nightmare from her college years that still pops up years later: She's in an upper-level math class, only to realize that she's halfway through the semester and has skipped class for weeks, leaving her woefully behind.

For this circle of listeners, God was clearly in the moment when Kelly followed her urge to look up. The beauty of creation—the trees, the sky, her body, her brain—all of this echoed Psalm 121, which says,

> I lift my eyes to the hills—
> from where will my help come?
> My help comes from the LORD,
> who made heaven and earth.
> —Ps. 121:1–2

DAY NINETEEN

Come Color with Us!

By Ellie, age thirteen, telling a story from her recent past

One Wednesday when I got home from school, I saw
my little sister and her best friend sitting at the table
drawing. "Come color with us!" they joyfully screamed.
Immediately I was extremely annoyed. I had planned on
doing the homework I had procrastinated on all week.
So I managed to say no in the nicest way possible and
went into the next room for some peace and quiet. In the
middle of doing my homework I realized how I would feel
if my friend's older sister said she wasn't going to color
with us when we were age six. So I peeled my attention
away from the paper due on Friday, and I trudged into
the kitchen where they were sitting. "I guess I can color
with you guys," I said, half meaning it and wishing I were
still doing my homework. Their eyes lit up the moment
I said that. For about half an hour, the three of us had
competitions to see who could finish drawing their picture first. When it came time for my little sister's friend to
leave, I was surprised that I didn't want her to go. I had

actually enjoyed coloring with two six-year-olds! That fact left an imprint on my mind, but what happened five minutes later, I will never forget.

In between leaving our house and getting into her mom's car, my little sister's friend had climbed up the tree next to our house. There were plenty of other kids in the tree who were playing in the homemade tree house with her. But while trying to hang upside down, my sister's friend lost her grip and plunged ten feet down, landing on her head. "Call 911!" shouted a petrified neighbor running into our house as fast as she could. When I stepped outside I heard the whispers of frightened neighbors and the faint sound of sirens in the background. When I turned my head, the mother, a certified nurse, was giving CPR to her own daughter. By the time the ambulances had arrived, the rest of her family and our whole street had, too. Her two sisters and I cried and cried when she was lifted onto a stretcher and into the ambulance.

The next day I learned that the six-year-old girl had broken her collarbone and had a concussion. The only thing she had remembered was coloring with my sister and me—nothing at all about climbing up the tree. But I remembered. I didn't want to dwell on how easily something much worse could have happened, so I comforted myself knowing that God had been protecting that little girl. I guess you never know how fast something can be taken away from you until it is almost gone. And you never realize the size of the impact on someone's life, no matter how small the deed, even if it is just coloring.

Practice L.I.V.E.

After you've heard Ellie's story, take a deep breath, and **LISTEN** to the responses it calls forth in you. Now **IMMERSE** yourself in the feelings it evoked. With whom did you identify in the story? Are you the older sister or the younger friend? Did you experience feelings of worry, dread, or relief as the story progressed? After you've sat for a few minutes with those feelings, begin to **VIEW IT WIDER.** Where is God in the story? Where is Scripture?

After sitting for a while with the **LISTENING, IMMERSING,** and **VIEWING IT WIDER,** ask yourself if there is a future emerging for you from this story. **EXPLORE** any actions or Aha! moments that it seems to stir up for you. What is there about this story or the way it made you feel about yourself or God that you want to continue pondering? What is there about this story and your reflection on it that helps you hear God speaking to your life today?

Take a moment to jot down answers to any of these questions and, especially, to remind yourself later of a story from your own life that this story called to mind.

What Others Experienced

Ellie told this story to her junior high youth group one Sunday night, just after they had been introduced to the L.I.V.E. method. A circle of Ellie's close friends sat around her, and they leaned into the story as she spoke, some of them fearing the worst. "I thought something really bad was going to happen," Samantha said, when Ellie was finished. "I'm so glad she was okay." Others had similar feelings and identified with Ellie's decision to put her homework aside in order to play.

The story reminded Hallie of a very different ending to a similar story. She briefly shared her memory, in which a little girl ran out in front of a car and was killed. For that reason, Ellie's story brought up some feelings of grief, sadness, and dread for Hallie. "Her death didn't have to happen," Hallie said. "It was senseless." We sat with those

BAD THINGS, GOOD PEOPLE

When Bad Things Happen to Good People is the title of an influential book written by a Jewish rabbi named Harold Kushner, who lost his fourteen-year-old son to disease (New York: Harper Collins, 1981). In the midst of Ellie's story with a happy ending, Hallie introduced a tragic memory, connected to deep grief and unanswered questions she still grapples with. Why do bad things happen to good people? Where is God when tragedy happens? Although it was important to make sure Ellie's story remained the focus of our time together, it was also vitally important to attend to Hallie's grief and the unanswered questions she brought about God's presence in the midst of tragedy. An adult in the group sought her out afterward and made a plan to spend time inviting her questions and talking more about stories that have unhappy endings. If you're interested in hearing more about Kushner and his wisdom, you can download an interview with him at www.npr.org/templates/story/story.php?storyId=124582959.

feelings for a moment before gently moving back to wondering where God is in Ellie's story.

Because stories like this one sometimes don't have happy endings, it was a story that stirred up wonderings about where God is when bad things happen. The earthquake in Haiti had just happened a week before, so the faces of people who had lost parents, siblings, or children were fresh in our minds. "God doesn't cause bad things to happen, but God is present to us in the midst of such hard times," their pastor said. There were nods of agreement.

Ellie turned the conversation toward how good it had felt to get lost—for half an hour—in the simple childlike act of coloring. "It was freeing, just to color. I lost track of all time." We talked about the importance of remembering to slow down and enjoy simple pleasures, even on our busy days.

"This story reminds me of the time when Jesus welcomed the little children," James said. "He took the time to slow down" (Mark 10:13). We talked about the importance of making decisions that honor our intuition to play—whether that's coloring, shooting hoops, or baking cookies. Abby jumped in with her Aha! moment: "I agree!" she said. "Next time, I'm going to put down my homework and play with my little sister!" We laughed, but she was serious. "There are too many times when I ignore her," she confessed.

As our conversation came to a close, we returned to the sad and scary reality of what "could have" happened. I mentioned a teenager I know who told me that she and her family members have a rule never to depart angry from one another. If they are having a hard time apologizing or letting go of an argument, they think of how they would feel if they never had a chance to do so. That always puts them in the mood to make up.

DAY TWENTY

The Rainbow Connection

By Angie, age thirty-two, recalling a season of her adolescence

I remember being called out of my class that day to report directly to the principal's office. My heart raced on my way down the hall, and I was dazed and confused as I tried to determine why the principal would want to see me.

When I turned the corner into the office I immediately noticed my older sister standing there, and I became even more perplexed. Then I saw him—not the principal but my father. He looked terrible; his countenance was strange and completely unfamiliar to me.

He didn't have to say a word. I knew then that she was gone. The doctors had diagnosed my twin sister with an acute form of leukemia just one month before this horrific day. We knew we needed a miracle. Although no miracle had occurred, we forced ourselves to find the minutest amount of comfort in the fact that she was no longer in extreme pain.

The days ahead were incredibly dark and practically unbearable.

As absurd as it may sound, my parents bought us a trampoline to bring some light and relief to our days. In and of itself, such a piece of equipment could certainly never do anything to ease the pain, but it truly did become a source of comfort. We spent endless hours soaring into the sky, jumping as high as possible. We learned daring tricks and bounced one another like cannon balls. The trampoline served as an outlet for bonding and entertainment with family, friends, and neighbors.

The trampoline also comforted me in a very special and personal way that I didn't share with anyone. One of the most traumatic aspects of losing my twin sister was the inability to have the opportunity to see her one last time and say good-bye. I just couldn't seem to get past it. If only I could have just one last day with her, a final chance to see her and tell her how much I loved her.

My deepest desire came true one night, as true as it will ever come this side of heaven. I had the most glorious dream of an entire day with Shelly. She came sliding down a rainbow from heaven straight to the trampoline! We jumped and laughed and played all day until it was almost dark. I dreaded her ascent back up the rainbow into the clouds, but I knew she had to go. I told her how much I loved her and said my final good-byes.

That dream, both healing and heartbreaking, was indescribably real. It will always remain among my most precious of memories, and I believe it was God's gift to bring me a sense of comfort and peace. From that night on, I felt a connection with Shelly and sensed her presence every time I stepped afoot on that trampoline.

Years later, the trampoline long gone, my older sister and I lay awake late one evening reminiscing about old times. She was home for a visit during her freshman year of college. Our conversation inevitably led to stories of Shelly, and we pondered what life might be like if she were with us. We laughed hysterically as we remembered her silly antics and crazy sense of humor. We speculated about her looks, her character and personality, her activities and goals.

It wasn't long before the discussion became serious, and we began to mourn her loss once again. For the first time, we expressed our frustrations concerning our parent's decision to have a closed-casket funeral. We had both yearned to see her one last time to bring closure to our life with her.

Then, my sister began to tell me about an incident that helped carry her through the difficulties of Shelly's death, something she had never before told anyone. It was a dream she once had, not long after Shelly died.

As she began to describe the dream to me, I sat there transfixed and practically paralyzed. Her voice was tearfully joyous as she said, "I had the most glorious dream of an entire day with Shelly. She came sliding down a rainbow from heaven straight to the trampoline! We jumped and laughed and played all day until it was almost dark. I dreaded her ascent back up the rainbow into the clouds, but I knew she had to go. I told her how much I loved her and said my final good-byes."

I have never been so awestruck as I was at that moment in my life. My heart raced as I sat there with tears streaming down my face, and I was dazed and confused as I stared at my sister. This was inconceivable. We knew we needed a miracle. A miracle had indeed occurred.

Practice L.I.V.E.

After you've read Angie's story, take a deep breath, and close your eyes. **LISTEN** to the responses it calls forth in you. **IMMERSE** yourself in the feelings it stirs up. If you've ever lost someone close to you, you may be brought directly in touch with Angie's grief. Allow yourself to feel this, remembering that grief is a normal part of every life and that you are in a safe space to experience it for a little while. What other emotions does this story touch? Is there a powerful dream from years ago that still burns in your memory? Have you ever spent an afternoon doing something carefree and fun, like jumping on a trampoline, with friends who could let you be entirely yourself?

Of what stories from your own life did this story remind you? With whom or what in the story did you identify?

After you've sat for a few minutes with those feelings, begin to **VIEW IT WIDER.** Wonder where God is in the story. When someone dies—especially a child or a sibling—it may feel for a while like God is far away. Are there stories from Jesus' life and ministry that this story calls to mind?

After sitting for a while **LISTENING, IMMERSING,** and **VIEWING IT WIDER,** begin to **EXPLORE** where this story might take you. Is there an action you've been pondering or a change you want to make in your world that seems related to this story or your reflections on it? What is there about this story and your reflection on it that helps you hear God speaking to your life today?

Take a moment to jot down answers to any of these questions and, especially, to remind yourself later of a story from your own life that this story called to mind.

What Others Experienced

A wide range of emotions were at the surface as Angie became silent. The utter sadness of losing a close sibling, particularly a twin, called forth a long period of empathy. Angie had kept this special memory close to her heart for many years, sharing it only with a few close friends. After she revisited these memories, there was a sacred feeling in the air, which we just kind of settled into as we passed around a box of tissue and let some tears fall.

After sharing feelings and stories of loss that the story recalled in us, we moved into focusing on dreams. We were all amazed that Angie and her sister had shared the same dream without knowing about it until years later. We named a sense of mystery that seemed to be wrapped up in the experience of that summer—the lightness of the trampoline in relief to the heaviness of their grief—and of the starlit night, years later, when the dreams were brought to speech.

A few people in the group told stories about powerful dreams, particularly of loved ones who had died. I told about a dream I still remember vividly. My grandfather, deceased a year, sat up in his hospital bed, dressed in one of his characteristically loud shirts, stretched his arms toward me, told me everything was okay, and enveloped me in a feeling of total warm acceptance. After that dream, I felt totally at peace about his loss, even though I hadn't been able to attend his funeral because I had just undergone surgery. We talked about the importance of closure when a loved one dies and moved back into reliving the feelings of Angie's inability to say good-bye to her twin sister.

When talk turned to Scripture, someone mentioned Joseph's dreams, dreams that held the power to save an entire kingdom and its neighbors from famine. Does God use our imaginations—our brains full of synapses, cells, and neurons—as a pathway to heal our emotions and comfort our deepest wounds? We spent a good deal of time also talking about the symbolism of the rainbow and the trampoline. Because it became a place to take her friends when they visited that summer, it reminded someone of the Jewish tradition of sitting shivah. Shivah is the seven days of mourning following a death, during which it is customary to visit the family. It seemed as if the trampoline

MORE ABOUT JEWISH CUSTOMS OF MOURNING

The Jewish tradition has much to teach other faiths about ways to be present with those who are mourning, because it emphasizes the importance of placing loss and grief in the context of community. Sometimes in the face of loss and death, we don't know what to say, how to act, or what to do. Tips for sitting shivah at the Web site www.myjewishlearning .com provide simple directions that can help people of any faith tradition make a visit more comforting to those who mourn and less intimidating for those who visit.

provided a passageway into another reality, a place where Angie could be visited by and cared for by her friends and, through the dream, also by her deceased sister. The dream reminded a few of us of what it must have felt like when Jesus ate fish with his friends on the beach following his death and resurrection.

Before telling the story in L.I.V.E., Angie had never shared this story with anyone, not even her own parents. Angie's Aha! moment was the decision to tell her parents about the comforting dream she and her sister shared.

DAY TWENTY-ONE

Bench Warming at Wal-Mart

*By Jason, age thirty-two, who also told "The Hummingbird"
story about his grandfather, at the beginning of this book. When
he tells the following story he is a few years older.*

A few weeks ago my grandparents went to a local Wal-Mart to pick up a few things. As they entered the store, my grandfather told my grandmother to go and get what she needed. He wanted to walk through the store and meet her later on in the middle. As my grandfather came down the center aisle of Wal-Mart, he saw a boy who was afflicted. His father was sitting on a bench with his head in his hands. As my grandfather walked past the boy, the boy asked my grandfather to sit on the bench with him.

So my grandfather did. He began to have a conversation with this young man. Every time the boy spoke, his father elbowed him, as if to say, "Be quiet!" Despite that, my grandfather kept talking with this boy. Eventually, the boy begin rubbing my grandfather's head and patting his hand as they talked.

After some time, my grandfather stood to go, explaining that it was time to find his wife. He said he would be back to say good-bye before he left. After he found my grandmother, he took her to meet the boy he had met on the Wal-Mart bench. The boy saw my grandfather coming and became very excited. He had a grin that filled his face! The father, who earlier didn't want his son speaking, approached my grandfather and expressed his thanks for my grandfather's taking the time to sit on a bench in Wal-Mart with his son.

It turns out that this "boy" was actually around the age of thirty and had a mental disability. While many others had passed by this young man, my grandfather stopped and took a few moments to visit with him, and it made all the difference in the world for that day.

Practice L.I.V.E.

After you've read Jason's story, take a deep breath, and close your eyes for a moment or two. **LISTEN** to the responses it calls forth in you. **IMMERSE** yourself in the feelings. What emotions stirred in you? Did you feel empathy for the father, the boy, or the grandfather? Did you wish the story would linger on or end sooner? Did you wish your life moved at a slower pace, so you, too, would notice the "boy"? Or are you fine leaving that role to a retiree?

Of what stories from your own life did this story remind you? With whom or what in the story did you identify?

After you've sat for a few minutes with those feelings, begin to **VIEW IT WIDER.** Wonder where God is in the story. Is church like a bench, where strangers meet for a moment of brief connection? Is God reflected in the image of the boy or the grandfather? What about Jason? He hears this story from his grandfather and takes note of something he might aspire toward. Who provides an example like that in your life?

After sitting for a while with the **LISTENING, IMMERSING,** and **VIEWING IT WIDER,** begin to **EXPLORE** where this story would take you. Is there an action you've been pondering or a change you want to make in your world that seems related to this story or your reflections on it? What is there about this story and your reflection on it that helps you hear God speaking to your life today?

Take a moment to jot down answers to any of these questions and, especially, to remind yourself later of a story from your own life that this story called to mind.

What Others Experienced

Jason's story evoked mixed emotions. One man in the group, Doug, shared memories of being raised with a sister who had Down syndrome. Although he had many happy memories of times spent with his sister, he also could remember "wanting to disappear" when he was seen in public with her during his teen years. He felt shame at this memory but a bit of relief, too, in naming it out loud. Karen felt admiration for the grandfather. He didn't walk on. He wasn't in a hurry.

Debra had a powerful memory that she shared in detail. A hushed silence fell as she shared with much emotion about a mission trip she had taken with her youth group to a home for disabled children. Early on in the visit she had bonded with a young man named Ben. During the day, they ate meals together, played games, and even danced. Although she had felt awkward and a little afraid at the beginning of the day, at one moment she experienced "knowing exactly why [she] had come" because of the welcome she gave and received from Ben. Clearly, as is often

WHAT IS THE L'ARCHE COMMUNITY?

L'Arche is an international movement to involve people of faith living and worshiping alongside developmentally challenged adults. Founded in France forty years ago, there are now one hundred and twenty L'Arche communities in eighteen countries. To listen to an interview with the founder of the movement, Jean Vanier, go to http://speakingof faith.publicradio.org/programs/2009/wisdom-of-tenderness/. For more stories about the L'Arche movement, see http:// speakingoffaith.publicradio.org/programs/larche/.

the case when we think we are "in mission," it became hard to tell the giver from the receiver. Both the young man on the bench and Jason's grandfather received the gift of God's presence that day at Wal-Mart.

When talk turned to Scripture, someone mentioned a passage from Hebrews 13:2, which we looked up. It reads, "Do not neglect to show hospitality to strangers, for by doing that some have entertained angels without knowing it." We also talked about Jesus' Sermon on the Mount, in which he says, "'Blessed are the meek, for they will inherit the earth'" (Matt. 5:5).

Someone was reminded of the life story of Henri Nouwen, a Roman Catholic theologian who spent much of his adult life living in a L'Arche community with mentally challenged people. L'Arche communities create homes where mentally challenged adults receive mutual respect and loving attention in family-like settings. Like Jason's grandfather on the park bench, people who've spent time in L'Arche communities find an openness to wonder and a welcome among developmentally delayed adults that are often missing from worlds too focused on achievement, success, and pursuits of the rational mind.

A SENDING FORTH

I hope you walk away from these stories with L.I.V.E. met-aphorically tucked into your back pocket. When you have an experience that moves you—a walk in the woods, a long talk with a friend, a sudden flash of insight that helps you solve a problem—take a deep breath and remember the practice of theological reflection. It's as simple as remembering the four steps: *LISTEN, IMMERSE, VIEW IT WIDER,* and *EXPLORE.*

I live my life differently because of these stories. I remember Adelle saying that when she feels distant from God, she turns toward whoever around her is suffering. I remember MK finding a seat on the bus, and I find a little more courage to take a risk on behalf of someone else. I think of Melissa walking the labyrinth, and I remember to kick off my flip-flops and open myself to an encounter with the Holy One.

Through listening to stories like these across the years, I've become convinced that our lives are like fifth Gospels. This notion, which helped us understand God's presence after Melissa told the story about those special moments with her mom, speaks to all these stories and to the art of reflecting on them in light of God's story.

Each of us is the pen with which God is writing a fifth Gospel, Judith Siqueira says. If that's true, God's story isn't finished. There are moments *in our own lives* when God continues to reveal God's self. These are our "little Gospels." When we cultivate awareness of them, we are apt to begin finding them more often. When shared with a circle of caring listeners, these little Gospels can help us confirm our hunches about who God is and where we might find God's story in our story. When we take a new action—even a seemingly small one—we open ourselves more to becoming who we are created to be.

Sometimes, in these tiny steps, we come to understand better just how our unique sets of gifts, talents, personalities, and desires might be exactly what's needed in a certain corner of the world. Derrick became a minister who is always thinking about how to draw a larger circle and invite people in. Brenda is a Christian educator who spends her days helping young people. Kelly teaches young teachers, celebrating with them moments when they see a new skill emerge in a student. Adelle keeps going back to Africa.

Each of the stories collected here holds a glimpse of God. Each story reminds us of the numerous stories of our own, all of them containing glimpses of God. If we learn to listen more deeply to our own lives, we find ourselves wondering about the small, seemingly insignificant moments: a kiss, a freed hummingbird, a chance encounter on a bench at Wal-Mart. When shared with a caring listener, these moments reveal patterns. They show us glimpses of ourselves that God may want us to notice, remember, ponder, or act on.

L.I.V.E. now belongs to you as a way of thinking about your life in light of God's dream for the world. Take it with you into your work, your play, your service, your worship. Kick off your flip-flops more often, and perhaps you'll begin to find little Gospels everywhere, leading you along the path of finding your purpose.

APPENDIX 1

Two Helpful Handouts

In what follows, you will find a reproducible handout that can help you lead the L.I.V.E. method with groups. The first page is a summary of each step of the method. The second page is a covenant that can be used at the beginning of each session, reminding participants of a few simple rules that help the group create safe space.[1]

1. Adapted from the Center for Courage & Renewal. Used by permission of the authors.

L.I.V.E.
A four-step practice
for theological reflection

Listen: Enter into a deep listening to the story. Ask yourself to listen with God's ears.

Immerse in the feelings: Name the feelings that emerged. Be sure to explore the whole spectrum, from ☺ to ☹ and everything in between. What stories from your own life does this story call to mind?

View it wider: Ask, "where is God in this story for me?" Remember stories from Scripture. Think of Christian practices, such as hospitality, grieving, protesting, lamenting, worshiping, etc. What does this story bring to mind from God's story?

Explore actions and Aha! moments: Ask yourself, "So what now?" What action might you take in the world as a result of this time with God and others? Name any Aha! moments.

From Dori Grinenko Baker, *The Barefoot Way: A Faith Guide for Youth, Young Adults, and the People Who Walk with Them* (Louisville, KY: Westminster John Knox Press, 2012), www.DORIBAKER.com

Covenants of Presence

Adapted from a document called "Touchstones" created by the Center for Courage &
Renewal and Parker J. Palmer. www.couragerenewal.org. Used by permission.

— **Be 100 percent present.** Set aside distractions. Welcome others into the story space, and presume you are welcome as well.

— **Listen Generously.** Listen intently to what is said and to the feelings beneath the words. As Quaker Douglas Steere writes, "To listen another's soul into life, into a condition of disclosure and discovery—may be almost the greatest gift we can offer to another." (*Gleanings: A Random Harvest* [Nashville: Upper Room, 1986], 73).

— **Author Your Story.** We all have a story. You might say, "I don't have a story or I don't have a story worth telling," but you do, and the world needs to hear it. Claim authorship of your own story, and learn to tell it so it can join a chorus that is part of God's ongoing story.

— **We come as equals.** We don't have the same gifts, limits, or experiences, but no person's gifts, limits, or experiences are more or less important than another's.

— **It is never "share or die."** The invitation to share in this process is completely by choice. You will determine the extent to which you want to participate.

— **No fixing.** We are not here to set someone else straight, right a wrong, or provide therapy. We are here to witness God's presence and movement in the sacred stories we share.

— **Suspend judgment.** Set aside your judgments. By creating a space between judgments and reactions, we can listen to another person, and to ourselves, more fully.

— **Turn to wonder.** If you find yourself becoming judgmental or cynical, try turning to wonder: "I wonder why she shared that story or made those choices?" "I wonder what my reaction teaches me." "I wonder what he's feeling right now."

— **Hold these stories with care.** There are many people who will benefit from the stories they hear during our time together. Imagine hearing another as you would listen to Scripture—attentively and mindfully, being open to the holy.

— **Be mindful and respectful of time.** We all have something important to share, and the discipline of time invites us to focus and make particular choices so that we might hear from everyone.

— **Practice confidentiality.** We create a safe space by respecting the nature and content of the stories heard. If anyone asks that a story shared be kept in confidence, the group will honor that request.

— **Believe that it is possible for us to emerge from our time together refreshed, surprised, and less burdened than when we came.**

APPENDIX 2

Frequently Answered Questions: A Guide for L.I.V.E. Group Leaders

1. When asking people to share stories of their own, it is helpful to have them write the story and share it with you in advance.
2. Once the storyteller is finished telling, participants should refrain from asking, "What happens next" questions, unless they are to clear up confusion.
3. Once the story is told, it belongs to the group. The purpose is not to figure out the meaning for the storyteller but for each person to find his or her own meaning in the story.
4. There shouldn't be pressure for everyone to come up with the same, shared meaning. Often stories hold diverse meanings and images.
5. The storyteller and facilitator are free to take part in the conversation.
6. It is best when leading a group of young people for more than one adult to be present.
7. It is also best for adults who are leading youth to make sure they don't speak too much. Allow the focus to remain on the meanings youth themselves are making, but feel free to share an important story, idea, or concept when the need arises.

8. The session can be as brief as twenty minutes or as long as ninety minutes. The facilitator should be clear about time limits at the start and guide people gently through each step in order to finish within the allotted time.
9. Almost any story will work with the L.I.V.E. process, but here are the guidelines I've found helpful:

— We are looking for a fresh, true, slice-of-life story that is about you and your experience. Try to use as much detail as possible, depicting sights, sounds, colors, smells, etc.
— Sometimes the first story that pops into your head is the one that wants to be told.
— The story should not be one you've told repeatedly in a group or therapeutic session. If you are in the midst of an extremely difficult crisis, tell that story to a pastor or counselor. Elements of such stories are usually still ongoing and are probably not ready to be shared in a setting like this.
— The story should not be about your religious conversion. In fact, the more explicitly religious language in the story, the less fun the process. Tell the story without giving us its meaning.

For a more detailed discussion of pastoral issues that arise in leading a method like this, see Dori Grinenko Baker, *Doing Girlfriend Theology: God-Talk with Young Women* (Cleveland, OH: Pilgrim Press, 2005).

This book is part of an approach to congregational life called VocationCARE. VocationCARE is an acronym that points to four communal practices:

C—Creating hospitable space to explore Christian vocation
A—Asking self-awakening questions
R—Reflecting theologically on self and community
E—Enacting next faithful steps

Resources that support VocationCARE include Web-based tools, videos, consultation, grants, conferences, retreats, and other learning events. An additional book— *Greenhouse of Hope: Congregations That Grow Young People Who Will Change the World,* ed. Dori Grinenko Baker (Herndon, VA: Alban Institute, 2010)—assists congregations in guiding vocational discernment with youth and young adults. To learn more about FTE, visit www.fteleaders.org.

Dori Baker
Calling Congregations
The Fund for Theological Education

CPSIA information can be obtained at www.ICGtesting.com
Printed in the USA
LVOW04s1327230814

400499LV00011B/285/P

9 780664 238025